SAILING

Bareboat Cruising

The national standard for quality sailing instruction

2ND EDITION

Acknowledgments

This book has been created by our talented team of designers, illustrators, photographer and writers. Anne Gram, freelance designer and cruising sailor, designed the page layouts. Mark Smith continued his involvement as design consultant to ensure the "look" he created with *Basic Keelboat* and *Basic Cruising* would be carried over into this book. Invaluable input and advice were provided by sailing schools, charter companies and volunteers, and there are a number of individuals who deserve special recognition: Tim Broderick, Steve Colgate, Judy Durant, David Forbes, Rich Jepsen, Richard Johnson, Timmy Larr, James Muldoon, Tyler Pierce, Anthony Sandberg, Susie Trotman, and Dr. William C. Waggoner. However, none of this would have been possible without the encouragement and financial support of SAIL AMERICA and US SAILING's Officers and Board.

Diana Jessie, *Writer*
Diana enjoys racing and cruising, and has completed a 60,000 mile circumnavigation. Thousands have attended her cruising seminars and read her articles in *SAIL, Sailing, Yachting* and *Yachting World*. At present, she lives and works (on a computer in the quarter berth) aboard her 48-foot sloop in San Francisco Bay. She and her marine surveyor husband Jim are preparing for another long cruise in 1996.

Shimon-Craig Van Collie, *Writer*
A dedicated sailor for the over 40 years, Shimon cruised and raced the waters of both the East and West coasts. As a sailing journalist, he covered sailing and boardsailing since 1979. Shimon was a regular contributor to Latitude 38, West Coast editor of *Sailing* magazine and authored the book *Windsurfing: The Call of the Wind*, published in 1992. He died tragically in 2000 of cancer. Sailing has lost a wonderful talent and a wonderful person.

Kim Downing, *Illustrator*
Kim grew up in the Midwest doing two things, sailing and drawing, so it's only natural that his two favorite pastimes should come together in the production of this book. He has been the technical illustrator for *SAIL* magazine since 1988 and is the proprietor of Magazine Art and Design, which provides technical illustrations for books and magazines worldwide. He and his family enjoy cruising and occasional racing on the Great Lakes aboard their 26 foot sailboat.

Rob Eckhardt, *Illustrator*
A graphic design professional, Rob is currently on the staff of *SAIL* Magazine and has many years of experience as a designer for advertising agencies, publications and his own business clients. He is a graduate of the Rochester Institute of Technology, Rochester, NY. Rob began sailing dinghies as a youngster and currently enjoys one-design racing and coastal cruising.

Chuck Place, *Photographer*
A professional photographer for seventeen years, Chuck has worked for a wide range of clients, including *National Geographic, Time, Smithsonian, Travel & Leisure* and *SAIL* magazines. Working out of a home base in Santa Barbara, CA, Chuck is able to combine his love for the ocean and images by photographing sailboats, one of his favorite subjects.

Tom Cunliffe, *Writer*
Tom brings his experience as professional sailor and RYA Yachtmaster Examiner to his writing. His articles appear in major periodicals and his books include a four book navigation series, *Easy on the Helm, Cunliffe on Cruising, Topsail and Battleaxe* and *Hand Reef and Steer*. These last two won BEST BOOK OF THE SEA prizes. He also finds time to cruise in his 35-ton Edwardian gaff cutter with his wife Ros and daughter Hannah to such diverse places as Brazil, Greenland, the Caribbean, the U.S., Labrador and Russia.

Foreword

I have spent many of the happiest days of my life cruising in my own or in chartered bareboats. So many of the books every sailor consumes are tales larger-than-life, by men and women of heroic mold. They are thrilling but too far beyond the average weekend or vacation sailor's experience to be really helpful. What I always needed was a book like this: a book for the "ordinary seaman."

Robert MacNeil

Robert MacNeil was Executive Editor and Co-anchor of The MacNeil/Lehrer Newshour on public television and has been an avid cruising sailor for many years.

Bareboat Cruising is part of US SAILING's Certification Series, which includes *Basic Keelboat, Basic Cruising, Bareboat Cruising, Coastal Navigation* and *Passage Making*. The Certification Series is based on the US SAILING programs that form the national standard for quality sailing instruction.

Photo courtesy The Moorings®

Part 4: Navigation

Part 5:
Health, Safety and Emergencies

Appendix

"Those who get the most out of charters are the people who remain flexible, who are willing to change their plans on a whim or with the weather, and who believe that getting there is less important than enjoying the trip."

Christopher Caswell, Marine Journalist

Planning Makes the Difference

A bareboat charter provides you with the opportunity to sail a boat on your own in an area of your choice. As a vacation, a bareboat charter offers the thrill of using your sailing skills, exploring new or favorite waters and spending time with friends and family.

Of course, any venture that involves moving people, supplies and equipment over both time and space requires planning. In fact, careful preparation for a bareboat charter can often spell the difference between a memorable success and a forgettable disappointment. At the same time, some spur-of-the-moment spontaneity adds extra spice to your trip. Having the basics covered, though, will ensure the foundations of a pleasant voyage.

Destinations. While you may not be able to reach all of the world's exotic ports on a bareboat charter, you can spend considerable time enjoying the Caribbean, the Bahamas, Mexico, the South Pacific, Australia, Northern Europe and the Mediterranean. Consider also destinations closer to home, such as California's Channel Islands, Maine's tree-lined coast, and Florida's Gulf Coast with its barrier islands.

Time of Year. Many people charter to take a break from their local weather. New Englanders will head for the Caribbean, for example, to escape the winter cold. A trip to Northern Europe could be a refreshing break from a hot southwestern summer. Expect to pay higher prices during the busy seasons. Low season bargains, such as summer on the sweltering Baja peninsula, may not be much fun at all. Your timing may be influenced by other weather factors and your competence to handle, for example, the 25 knot "Christmas winds" that frequent the Caribbean winter.

Type of Sailing Area. If you want to spend a majority of your time sailing, you might pick an area where anchorages are spaced far apart and offer a variety of upwind and downwind configurations. If you want to spend more time swimming, snorkeling, exploring or relaxing, consider locations where anchorages are within easy sailing distance of one another, such as the Virgin Islands. Remote areas, such as the Grenadines, are beautiful, but they don't offer the bright lights of St. Thomas.

Companions. Sharing costs with another couple, family or friends may make a bareboat charter more affordable. Before doing so, consider some other questions: Is everyone compatible under close living situations?

Does anyone have any special health considerations? Do you enjoy the same food and music? Do you want to appreciate nature on your trip or spend the evenings singing and dancing? How will you be sharing expenses on the trip itself? Plan a pre-cruise tryout to get acquainted and answer some of these questions.

Non-Sailing Interests.
Many charterers seek to combine sailing with other activities, including shopping and sampling local foods. Snorkeling and scuba diving rank high for those going to tropical locations and charter companies offer packages or contacts to make planning easier. Exploring ancient ruins, museums and monuments or simply mingling with people of a different culture can be rewarding. Preplanning becomes even more important so you have the right equipment and target the best places for these activities.

Skill Level of the Crew. On your first charter to an unfamiliar location, you'll need to factor in the experience level of the crew. Different charter areas pose unique navigational and sailing challenges, including shoals, fog, proximity to shipping lanes and tropical storms. The British Virgin Islands offer predictable winds, short distances between destinations and easy anchoring. The Mediterranean, on the other hand, presents constantly changing wind patterns, crowded anchorages and the challenge of foreign languages.

Photo courtesy Sunsail

"No longer is the average sailor confined to the water he can reach in his own boat in the given time available... now the whole world, almost, if not literally, is his oyster in making plans for cruising."

Bill Robinson,
Former Editor, *Yachting* Magazine

A World of Possibilities

Each charter destination offers its own special aspects. You may have nursed a life-long fantasy to loll on a snow-white beach in Tahiti or climb the ruins of the Parthenon. Advance research will inform you how to fulfill those dreams or where to go for new adventures. Travel books, boating magazines and charter company brochures are good places to start. Charter brokers with firsthand experience can advise you on appropriate choices that suit your needs and experiences. Other sailors who've chartered can also be helpful.

If you've never been to your charter destination, there are a few factors to keep in mind as you plan your trip.

Climate. If you want hot, tropical weather, aim for a spot near the equator, which is warm all year. As you head farther north or south, expect cooler weather with seasonal changes. Make sure that your trip coincides with a favorable time of the year at your destination.

Experience. Sailing skill is one factor in choosing your first charter. Will you feel comfortable handling the boat in the waters and winds of your charter area? Are you confident enough in your anchoring skills to sleep through the night? Consider also that you may be in a foreign country with its unfamiliar language and customs.

Affordability. In addition to the boat, your charter costs will include transportation, pre- and post-cruise lodging, food (on board and dining out), extra equipment, additional supplies such as cooking gas, water and incidentals. To ensure a good time, leave extra room in the budget for the unexpected.

U.S. East Coast. Good sailing waters can be found on the east coast from the southern tip of the Florida Keys to the northern tip of Maine, the Chesapeake Bay and inland on

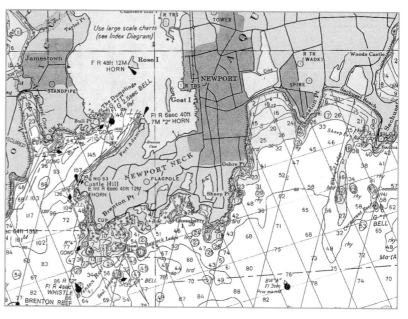

Newport, RI is a well known New England sailing center.

the Great Lakes. The more northerly climates feature excellent summer weather, but you'll want to go further south to areas like the Gulf Coast of Florida in the winter.

U.S. West Coast. The rugged Pacific coastline offers a variety of opportunities near the busy harbors of San Diego, Los Angeles and San Francisco as well as coastal and island destinations such as the Channel Islands off Santa Barbara, CA. You'll also find an abundance of protected waterways extending from Seattle's Puget Sound north to the inland passage of Alaska.

Caribbean. The most popular charter area in the world, the Caribbean possesses many

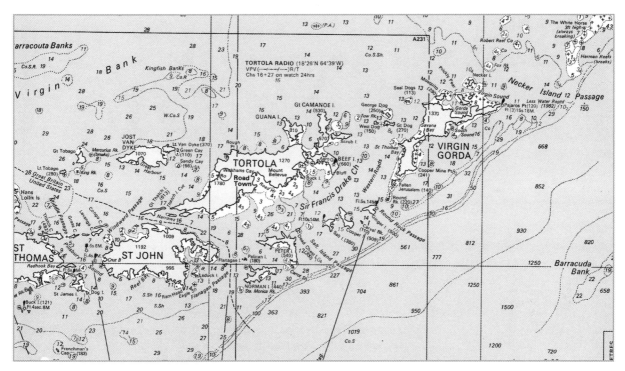

Caribbean islands such as Tortola are the most popular charter areas in the world.

attractive features, including easy access from the United States and Europe, warm and protected waterways, safe anchorages and a colorful infusion of cultures from both sides of the Atlantic. The Virgin Islands are ideal for first time charterers.

Peak sailing season in the Caribbean runs from December through May, with steady trade winds from the southeast. Substantial discounts may be available during the off season.

Other Areas. Good bareboat chartering can be found in many other areas of the world, with reputable charter companies there to serve you.

Europe. The waters of the Atlantic around northern Europe and the Mediterranean present a wide array of sailing options. Most chartering takes place during the summer months. July and August in the Mediterranean can sometimes bring strong

melteme and mistral winds, but they are followed by excellent sailing weather in the fall.

South Pacific and Asia. Tahiti, Tonga and Fiji support an active charter industry. These islands enjoy a dry season with steady trade winds and occasional tropical squalls from early May to late October. Other areas, including New Zealand, Australia and Thailand, enjoy warm weather during North America's cold winter months.

CHECKLIST

▶ Make sure your charter trip coincides with good sailing weather at your destination.

▶ Match your destination with your sailing skills and your budget.

▶ Research the area you want to visit beforehand to determine where you'd like to spend the bulk of your time and what you'd like to do while you're there.

▶ Consult with charter companies or brokers for information about the locations they serve.

Cruise Planning

An integral part, and part of the fun, of any cruise is planning for it. Like diners at a restaurant, you and your fellow sailors peruse the menu of options and pick what looks most appealing. Preparing for a bareboat charter includes responsibilities, too, since you will not only be the consumers of your feast, but also the cooks!

You'll need time to check out the boat before you can depart on your first day. Conversely, you'll have to check the boat in and leave it clean and shipshape before you can begin your

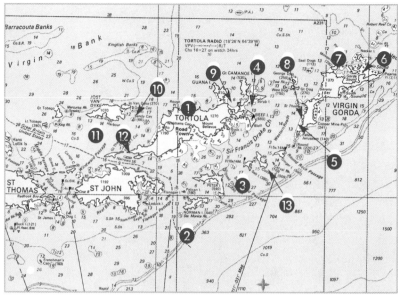

Imray-Iolaire chart courtesy Imray Laurie Norie and Wilson Ltd

Use charts of the area you'll be visiting to actually map out your proposed cruise (see Sample Schedule on facing page).

COMPATIBILITY CHECKLIST

▶ Make sure there's enough room on board to allow each crew member some privacy.

▶ Don't mix smokers and non-smokers or people with widely different expectations for the cruise.

▶ Include at least two competent sailors in case of an emergency. Encourage them to share their knowledge with others on board.

▶ Look for crew with mild tempers and healthy senses of humor.

▶ Give yourselves a trial run with a pre-cruise trip or meeting to verify your compatibility.

trip home. If traveling across national boundaries, allow for clearing customs and other official duties. As sailors, your trip will be dependent at least in part on variables such as wind and weather. Consider a bad weather route in addition to an optimal one.

Mapping Out Your Cruise. Factor in the tides, currents, prevailing wind directions and strengths and any special obstructions you may encounter. Leave yourself enough time during the day to swim, fish, go ashore, explore and relax. If your crew includes young children, allow time for rest and schedule activities with them. If you map out an easy downwind cruise, allow enough time for the return beat.

Do's & Don'ts

▶ Do make travel arrangements well in advance.

▶ Do leave some extra time in your itinerary and dollars in your budget.

▶ Do use up-to-date charts and guides when making your plans.

▶ Do note stopover points where you can refresh supplies, including food and water, or pump out the holding tank, if needed.

▶ Do make back-up plans for adverse wind and weather conditions.

▶ Do make sure everyone knows beforehand about special medical conditions that may exist among the crew and the procedures for handling any situations that may arise.

▶ Don't over-plan.

Length and Destinations

The length of your cruise will hinge on the time you have available. Your first inclination may be to cover as many miles as possible, leading you to map out an ambitious schedule. For a group of hearty voyagers, this may be an ideal vacation. For those who want to relax and indulge in non-sailing activities, a heavy sailing schedule will diminish their pleasure. For most cruises, figure on a maximum of three to five hours of sailing a day, scheduled during the periods of good wind strength (see example at bottom right).

CHECKLIST FOR EXTRA COSTS

► Restaurant meals, drinks and shopping
► Additional fuel, water and ice
► Moorings and dockage
► Guides, tours and scuba diving
► Customs and Immigration fees
► Gratuities
► Local taxes
► Airport / marina transfers

CHARTERING SMART...
Carry passport, essentials and medications in a carry-on bag. Luggage can get lost.

Sample Schedule

Day 1 Fly to **1** Tortola, British Virgin Islands, and check into local hotel arranged by charter company.

Day 2 **Morning** - check out boat and complete paperwork, stow personal items, have lunch on board. **Afternoon** - sail 6 miles to The Bight **2** on Norman Island, anchor, swim, dinner on board.

Day 3 **Morning** - breakfast on board, raise anchor and sail 7 miles to **3** Salt Island, pick up mooring, snorkel or dive the wreck of the Rhone, lunch on board. **Afternoon** - sail about 6 miles to **4** Marina Cay, anchor, snorkel, dinner on board.

Day 4 **Morning** - breakfast on board, raise anchor and sail 5 miles to **5** The Baths, Virgin Gorda, snorkel and explore ashore, lunch on board. **Afternoon** - sail 9.5 miles to **6** Bitter End Yacht Club, pick up mooring, dinner ashore.

Day 5 **Morning** - breakfast on board, explore and snorkel Eustacia Sound by dinghy, lunch on board. **Afternoon** - drop mooring and sail to **7** Drake Anchorage, Mosquito Island, explore ashore, dinner on board.

Day 6 **Morning** - breakfast on board, raise anchor, sail about 8 miles to **8** Virgin Gorda Yacht Harbor, tie up, buy bread and ice, lunch ashore or on board. **Afternoon** - sail about 14.5 miles past Little Camanoe and down the north side of Tortola to **9** Cane Garden Bay, dinner ashore at Stanley's or Rhymer's.

Day 7 **Morning** - breakfast on board, sail 3 miles to **10** Sandy Key, snorkel and walk nature trail, lunch on board. **Afternoon** - sail 2.5 miles to **11** Great Harbor, Jost van Dyke, visit Foxy's!

Day 8 **Morning** - breakfast on board, sail 5 miles to **12** West End, Tortola, stop for lunch at Pusser's. **Afternoon** - sail about 12 miles to **13** Cooper Island, pick up mooring, snorkel, captain's barbecue on board.

Day 9 **Morning** - return to charter company base in Roadtown, Tortola before noon, clean boat and check it in, take transport to airport for flight home.

How far can we cruise in a day?

If you assume an average speed of 5 knots (nautical miles per hour) for 4 hours, the daily cruising range will be 20 miles.

D (distance) = **S** (speed) x **T** (time) = 5 knots x 4 hours   **D** = 20 miles

If you're sailing into the wind or against a strong current, assume an average speed of 3 knots, which will reduce your range to 12 miles.

Selecting a Charter Company

As a potential customer, you can contact several charter companies to determine the best service for your charter requirements. Ask friends who have used the companies you're considering for their opinions. Look for professional practices and a business-like attitude at all levels of contact. Make sure that you have a complete understanding of the financial arrangements.

Equipment varies between companies. Be very clear about the equipment included in your contract and look for what's not listed. If there's no mention of a dinghy with outboard, for example, expect to pay extra.

WHAT TO BRING

Your gear should fit into a soft, water-resistant seabag. For warm weather sailing, include light cotton clothing, a wide-brimmed hat, plenty of sunscreen, polarized sunglasses and a lightweight windbreaker. Bring several bathing suits, a beach towel, shorts, T-shirts, long sleeve shirts for sun protection and sandals or sneakers for walking on coral or rocky beaches. For cooler weather areas, bring foul-weather gear, a warm sweater or jacket, long underwear, a knit cap and sea boots. For dinner ashore, you may need a dressy outfit. Bring a shirt and pants or blouse and skirt for locations where local custom or religion frowns on skimpy or inappropriate attire. Other personal items include a camera, plenty of film, music cassettes or CDs, plastic zipper bags, a video camera (with a back up battery in case you can't find power), books, games and plastic bags for dirty laundry. For kids, bring a few special toys, books and drawing gear.

SELECTION CHECKLIST

▶ Compare charter prices and total package cost including airfare, lodging, deposits, insurance, cancellation and refund policies, especially for lost sailing time due to equipment failure.
▶ Check provisioning options and costs.
▶ Compare included equipment, such as dinghy and outboard, barbecue, snorkel gear, sailboard, navigation tools, charts and guides, linens, etc.
▶ Check references and referrals, years in business.

Contracts and Deposits.

All charter companies require a deposit with your reservation. Your contract will specify the boat you reserved, the payment schedule, company refund practices, and any additional fees. Most companies require a security deposit or insurance to cover damage to the vessel. In some situations the deposit must be made in cash or certified check. Consider vacation insurance in case your charter is canceled.

DOCUMENT CHECKLIST

▶ Passport and Visa
▶ Traveler's checks, credit card and some cash
▶ US SAILING Bareboat Cruising Certification and Logbook

When You Arrive

Before you set out on your cruise, the charter company will verify your competence, usually by means of an oral quiz, or possibly an on board check out. Your US SAIL-ING Certification and Logbook will facilitate this process. In many areas, you have the option of hiring a charter captain, which often makes the first trip easier. If the charter company questions your expertise, they may put a captain on board, but the charterer still retains responsibility for the vessel.

Do's & Don'ts

▶ Do mark personal boat equipment that you bring on board.

▶ Do ask about unfamiliar gear or equipment.

▶ Don't forget that most charter companies manage privately-owned boats or boats leased from individuals. Treat their property gently and with respect.

Allow plenty of time to thoroughly inspect the boat and complete the check out checklist to ensure it has all the contracted items.

CHECK OUT THE BOAT

When you accept the boat, you assume responsibility for having the proper gear on board and for anything that you break or wasn't noted before departure. Record any defects or problems. Bring a portable tape recorder to note information at the boat check out and chart briefing. The water and fuel tanks should be full and the holding tank empty. Familiarize yourself with the propane stove operation and charcoal barbecue before you leave. Many charter companies have an operations manual or "boat book" on board that includes information on the systems and recommended procedures.

Review the boat systems, including engine operation, handling the cooking fuel, and the location of the master switch and electrical panel.

Check the ground tackle and get briefed on the safe operation of a windlass.

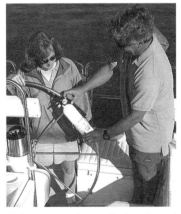

Make sure you know the location of emergency gear, through-hull fittings, and fire extinguishers.

Provisioning

Meals and food can be very enjoyable parts of your cruising experience. Charter companies offer a variety of provisioning plans and menus, and each boat has a slightly different galley plan and equipment. The easiest approach may be to opt for full provisioning provided by the charter company. Alternatively, you can hire an independent professional provisioner. There may also be items that you'll want to bring along or buy en route.

If you provision yourself, unload and remove paper bags and boxes immediately as they often carry insects or their eggs.

Provisioning Choices

Full - usually means three meals per day plus a snack and some beverages. It may also provide only three or four dinners for a week's cruise.

Partial - most often means breakfast, lunch and afternoon snack, with all dinners ashore. Sometimes it will include one to three dinners.

Custom or Individual - food is selected from expanded menus and accommodates special diets and groups desiring more than one entree.

Basic - includes only staples such as cooking oil, soap, paper products, and condiments for self-provisioning or to complement your other selection.

Alcohol and soft drinks are usually extras and their costs may range from cheap to remarkably expensive. Self-provisioning requires exact menu planning and sufficient quantities to satisfy your crew. Plan on large portions in cooler climates or longer passages and at least a half a gallon of drinking water per day per person.

Do's & Don'ts
▶ Do allow for dining out. Sampling local food is part of the fun.
▶ Don't forget special dietary needs.
▶ Do keep cooking simple so you have time to play.
▶ Do review sample menus with your companions before your cruise.

Lush pineapples in the Virgin Islands, fresh lobsters in Maine — these are part of the lure of cruising. Familiarize yourself with the storing, handling and preparation of local delicacies. Freshly picked produce will not require refrigeration, but fresh meat and dairy products will, especially in tropical climates.

What To Take. Most charter companies really do provide complete provisioning and will go out of their way for special requests. Nevertheless, you may want to bring some favorite spices or herbs, a special brand of soda or a particular bottle of wine which may not be available or may be prohibitively expensive in your charter area.

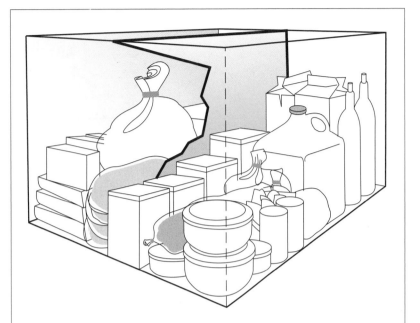

If you are stowing your own provisions, pack them in your refrigerator/ice box carefully and in the reverse order of use. Stow the most frequently wanted items, like ice water and cold drinks in a separate cooler or in the most accessible location in the refrigerator. Freeze spoilable items such as meat or fish and place them in the bottom of a top loading refrigerator. Make sure to keep perishables, such as lettuce, away from refrigeration cold plates. Always wedge opened containers with covers in an upright position. Fresh eggs need no refrigeration, but those bought from cold storage in the supermarket do.

LOCAL SHOPPING TIPS

▶ Buy only what you can use immediately.
▶ Limit your purchases to food that can be peeled or cooked.
▶ Bring local currency in small denominations.
▶ Bring your own string, straw or plastic bags.

You'll get a taste of local foods and culture at the market.

Restrictions and Breakdowns

Every charter company wants to provide you with a carefree voyage. Nevertheless, you may encounter unexpected situations. A good charter company will have instructions and offer assistance when things go awry, whether it's simply starting an outboard engine or supplying you with a different boat. At the boat check out, clarify what procedures you should follow. Be prepared and know what to do if you need help.

Handling Equipment Breakdowns. If items break or fail to function properly after a reasonable number of attempts, contact the charter office. In most locales you will call on a VHF radio using the designated channel or go ashore and use a telephone. Be prepared to give specific information about your problem, what action you took, and where you are located.

If you need to contact the charter company about a problem, the standard procedure is to call on Channel 16 and then switch to Channel 68 or another designated channel. If a charter company doesn't have VHF pick up or they're out of range, then go ashore and use a phone line. Some charter companies equip their boats with cellular phones.

WHEN TO CALL
(A SAMPLE CHECKLIST)

▶ engine fails to turn over after you have checked the battery charge and the battery switch
▶ engine fails to start after you have checked the fuel level and the kill switch
▶ engine overheats
▶ refrigeration goes off
▶ head will not pump
▶ dinghy disappears
▶ furling system freezes
▶ anchor windlass doesn't operate
▶ sails are torn or damaged
▶ steering system fails
▶ anchors or rodes are lost or damaged
▶ through-hull fittings are damaged or inoperable

RESTRICTIONS CHECKLIST

Charter contracts usually have a restrictions clause. Typical restrictions are:
▶ avoid unapproved sailing areas
▶ use only specified anchorages
▶ sail or motor only during daylight hours

Returning Your Boat

Most charters end at mid-day, so plan your return accordingly or you may risk additional charges or doing the clean-up work yourself. Have your crew packed and ready to disembark when you reach the charter dock. During the check in, note any signs of developing problems. Many charter companies will send a diver to inspect the bottom. Their staff will also go over the sails, engine and other systems while you're still there. Any damage incurred during your charter will be deducted from your security deposit.

Return your boat on time and in good condition so it will be ready for the next charter. Clean both below and above decks, including a fresh water rinse to remove salt and dirt. You should respect local water restrictions.

CHECKLIST

▶ Remove all personal gear and garbage from the boat.

▶ Turn off main battery switch and close the seacocks unless otherwise instructed.

▶ Follow charter company's instructions for dealing with unused provisions.

▶ Prepare a written list of damaged or worn equipment for the charter company so they can fix it for the next charterer.

▶ Return logs, permits or other documents provided for your charter to the charter office.

▶ Request a written receipt from the charter company to confirm the return of the boat.

Engine Management

Nearly all modern cruising boats use auxiliary engines for propulsion as well as charging batteries for lights, refrigeration, radio and other systems. While these pages present generic information, engines vary greatly, so it's important to adhere to the manuals, check out instructions and "boat books" you receive for your charter boat. Informed operation and simple daily engine inspections will make your cruising more carefree.

1 **Cap** (*deck plate*) marked "fuel" indicates where fuel should be pumped into the tank.

2 **Vent** in the fuel tank allows air to escape outside the boat when filling the tank.

3 **Primary fuel filter** collects impurities/separates water from fuel

4 **Fuel pump** moves the fuel into the engine.

5 **Throttle lever** controls the fuel flow.

6 **Engine stop control** (*kill lever/switch*) turns off fuel flow to the diesel engine.

7 **Engine block** houses the cylinders and fuel injectors (diesel) or spark plugs (gasoline).

8 **Dipstick** indicates quantity and condition of oil.

9 **Oil filler cap** permits adding oil when indicated on the dipstick.

10 **Coolant cap** allows addition of water or coolant if there is no header tank.

11 **Seacock** lets raw-water flow in.

12 **Raw-water strainer** filters and collects debris.

13 **Raw-water intake system** includes a pump with a rubber impeller that circulates seawater to cool the engine and exhaust gases.

14 **Lift can** combines raw-water with exhaust gases to cool engine exhaust.

15 **High loop** helps prevent water backflow into the engine.

16 **Exhaust outlet** is working properly when water flows out. If there is no water, turn off the engine immediately and check raw-water intake system. Make sure the seacock is open and filter is clean. Check the pump impeller.

17 **Batteries** provide the electricity for lights, instruments, starting the engine and, on some boats, the refrigeration.

18 **Alternator** generates electricity to charge the batteries.

19 **Transmission** transfers engine power to the propeller shaft and changes its direction to forward, reverse or neutral.

20 **Linkage** connects lever controls to the transmission.

21 **Starter motor** turns flywheel to start engine.

DAILY CHECKLIST

- ▶ Oil level, add if indicated.
- ▶ Coolant, add if indicated.
- ▶ Belts should be snug, look for signs of wear.
- ▶ Raw-water seacock is open.
- ▶ Raw-water filter, clean out debris.
- ▶ Engine pan and bilge for fuel, water or oil.
- ▶ Engine control levers for smooth operation.
- ▶ Stern gland (shaft seal, stuffing box, packing gland).

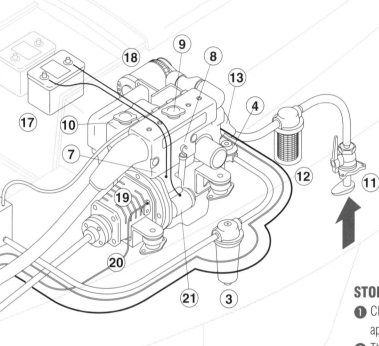

STARTING PROCEDURE

1 Check "boat book" or manuals to determine what steps are appropriate.

2 Complete daily checklist.

3 Turn battery switch to correct setting.

4 Engage engine blower (if gasoline).

5 Put engine stop control in RUN position.

6 Put gear in NEUTRAL, throttle slightly open.

7 Preheat (if diesel) with glow-plug control for 10-30 seconds.

8 Turn on ignition (oil pressure alarm should sound) and start engine.

9 Throttle engine to steady idle (oil pressure alarm should stop).

10 Check exhaust for consistent water flow.

11 Check gauges (oil pressure, water temperature, ammeter).

STOPPING PROCEDURE

1 Check "boat book" or manuals to determine what steps are appropriate.

2 Throttle to idle.

3 Shift to NEUTRAL!

4 Put engine stop control in STOP position.

5 Return engine stop control to RUN position after engine stops.

6 Turn ignition key to OFF position.

7 Put transmission in reverse while sailing to prevent shaft spinning.

HOW TO SWITCH BATTERIES

1 Set battery switch to the desired position (1,2 or ALL) before starting the engine or turning on the lights.

2 When batteries are low, start engine with master battery switch in the ALL position.

3 Change master battery switch position with the engine off unless the manufacturer's label indicates the contrary. Newer switches may have different instructions.

Most battery switches have four designations: 1,2, ALL (BOTH) and OFF. Typically, 1 or 2 designate either the "house" battery system or the engine starting system. ALL (BOTH) turns on both battery systems and OFF shuts them down. You may also find a separate engine battery switch on the electrical panel or elsewhere. Clarify battery switch designations during the check out.

NOTE: Passagemakers and long-distance cruisers who require a more in-depth knowledge of boat systems should reference US SAILING's Passage Making

MSD (Head)

Brief everyone aboard on the operation of the head and the rest of the MSD to prevent clogging or break-down of this critical system. Since several people may use the same head, stress tidying the area after each use. Ask your charter agent about disposal regulations in your charter area and the location of local pumpout stations before you depart.

Do's & Don'ts

▶ Do make sure everyone knows how to use the head properly before leaving the dock.

▶ Don't put anything into the head except a small quantity of toilet paper or something that has been swallowed first.

▶ Don't continue pumping when you encounter resistance.

▶ Do make sure all valves and seacock(s) are open before using.

▶ Don't forget to close valves and seacock(s) after using.

▶ Do leave area clean for the next person.

A TYPICAL CHARTER BOAT HEAD SYSTEM

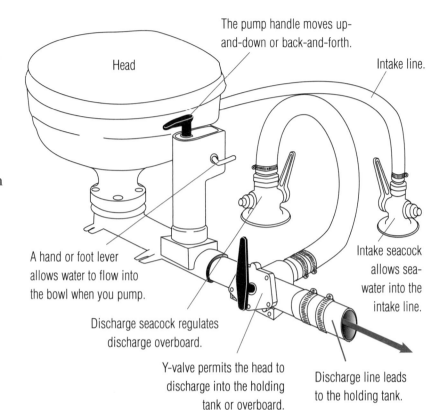

The pump handle moves up-and-down or back-and-forth.

Head

Intake line.

A hand or foot lever allows water to flow into the bowl when you pump.

Discharge seacock regulates discharge overboard.

Intake seacock allows sea-water into the intake line.

Y-valve permits the head to discharge into the holding tank or overboard.

Discharge line leads to the holding tank.

HEAD OPERATION CHECKLIST

1. Open raw-water seacock.
2. Open valve to holding tank or discharge seacock as required.
3. Depress hand or foot lever and pump a small amount of water into bowl before using.
4. Depress hand or foot lever to flush, and pump until bowl is clear. Then pump additional strokes to make sure discharge line is clear.
5. Release hand or foot lever and pump bowl dry.
6. Close all valves, seacock(s) and toilet lid after use.

This head has a twist knob located below the pump handle to control water flow into the bowl.

Manually operated heads may have a foot lever. Depress the pedal to let water in and release it to stop.

Photo courtesy Groco

Electrical System

Cruising for several days or weeks requires careful management of the boat's batteries and electrical system. Charter boats may have 115 or 220 volt AC electrical systems as well as the 12 volt DC battery system, so learn which type of electricity powers what fixtures. You won't be able to use the AC appliances or fixtures unless you are plugged into shore power or your boat has an inverter to change DC battery power into AC current.

The electrical control panel distributes the power to different functions on the boat. The switches on the panel are normally labeled by uses. Typically, you'll find the master battery switch, which controls the DC battery power, and the AC circuit breaker in the same area.

BATTERY CHECKLIST

1. Locate the batteries and check the fluid levels.
2. Make sure battery terminals show no signs of corrosion. Cables should be secure on posts.
3. Check the master battery switch position before starting engine.
4. If the engine battery charge is low, set the master battery switch to ALL (BOTH). This may give you enough power to start the engine.

AC appliances, such as blenders, hair dryers and AC light fixtures use AC current provided by a shore powerline or an inverter. Remember to run the engine to charge the batteries if you use an inverter.

DC-powered interior lighting, navigation lights, electronics, and the engine starter motor all run on the DC current from your batteries.

Do's & Don'ts

► Do monitor your battery condition through the voltmeter.

► Do turn off electrical fixtures and instruments when not in use.

► Do run engine daily to charge batteries unless using shore power.

► Don't use your engine battery for running "house" systems.

► Don't reposition the master battery switch with the engine running without first checking the electrical system manual.

Foreign Battery Systems

Foreign charter boats may have 24 or 32 volt DC systems and 220 volt, 50 cycle AC systems. If you take appliances with you, be sure you have the proper plugs and converter kits. The master battery switches may be different on a foreign yacht even when it is equipped with a 12 volt battery. Always ask if you are uncertain about the type of electricity or how the system operates.

Fresh Water

Charter boats carry limited fresh water and in many locations there is a charge for refilling. Familiarize yourself with the water system in the galley, the heads, and the on-deck shower. The pressure to produce a continuous flow of water relies on battery power, so caution everyone to turn off unused faucets and valves. When you're all on deck or turned in for the night, turn off the fresh water pump at the electrical panel. Some boats have manual water pressure in the head and galley that operates by foot or hand pumping.

There are several deck plates on most boats. Be sure you fill the one marked "water," not "waste" or "fuel."

FRESH WATER CHECKLIST

▶ Locate filler deck plate and control valves for water tanks.
▶ Turn off pressure water switch when everyone is on deck or retired for the night, and when you leave the boat unattended.
▶ Close valves and faucets when not in use.
▶ Draw from one tank at at time.

Boats often have a pressure water system (top) with faucets and a manual pump system (bottom) at the same sink. To conserve water, use the manual pumping system rather than the pressure system. Extend your fresh water supply by using salt water for washing dishes and showering, followed by a fresh water rinse.

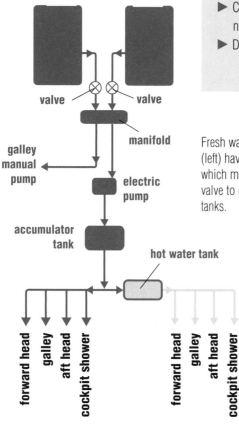

Fresh water systems on larger boats (left) have two or more water tanks, which may be connected by hoses and a valve to control the flow between the tanks.

Tank   **Tank**

valve   valve

manifold

galley manual pump

electric pump

accumulator tank

hot water tank

forward head / galley / aft head / cockpit shower   forward head / galley / aft head / cockpit shower

Regularly check water tank level.

Bilge and Through-hull Systems

Check out the bilge system carefully when you review the boat with the charter staff. Test the operation of all bilge pumps and ask what is "normal" bilge water before accepting your charter boat. Draining ice boxes and certain types of stern glands produce some bilge water during normal operation. Your charter agent may direct you to close all galley and head through-hulls when underway.

Each through-hull fitting should be labeled to indicate its use and have a wooden plug for emergencies.

Keep intake screen free of debris to prevent clogging the bilge pump. A float switch activates the automatic bilge pump. A clogged switch will cause the pump to run continuously and to burn out.

Locate and test the operation of the manual bilge pump.

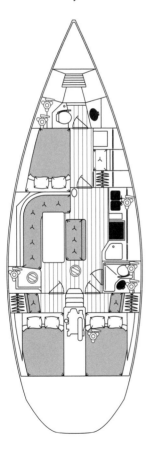

If there's no diagram of the through-hull fittings and bilge pump locations, make one of your own (see above).

BILGE CHECKLIST

► Determine whether the automatic bilge pump switch bypasses the main battery switch and goes directly to the battery by lifting the float switch when the main battery switch is turned off. The pump will start unless it's wired through the main battery switch.

► Locate and operate each through-hull valve.

► Check intake screens regularly.

► Clear debris from bilge that would lodge in float switch.

► If an unusual amount of water is in the bilge, taste it to determine if its source is fresh or salt.

► Monitor automatic pump if it does not have an alarm. Continuous operation indicates trouble.

Galley

A happy cruise relies on a good galley. Refrigeration, stoves with ovens, and pressurized water make cooking easy and convenient. Refrigeration requires power, so you'll need to run the engine daily to charge the batteries or to run a belt driven compressor-type refrigerator. Optional equipment often includes barbecues for outdoor cooking and ice chests for warm climates.

GALLEY TIPS

► For easy access, store provisions in the reverse order of planned consumption.

► Unlock stove gimbals underway and in active anchorages.

► Provisions may shift while underway, so be careful when you open lockers during or after a sail.

► Wear shoes when cooking underway and avoid wearing long sleeves or flowing garments.

► If you turn on the propane tank valve and the stove doesn't light, check that you have turned on the solenoid switch as well.

► If you have a fire on the propane stove, turn off the solenoid first.

► When using an alcohol stove, keep a sauce pan of water in the sink to douse an accidental fire.

Galley lockers should be fastened securely when underway. Stow heavy items such as canned goods and pots as low as possible. Avoid towers of canned goods in any locker because they fall and shift.

Top loading refrigerators and ice boxes stay colder longer than front opening models. To keep the cold in, minimize opening the ice box by getting all the items for a meal at one time.

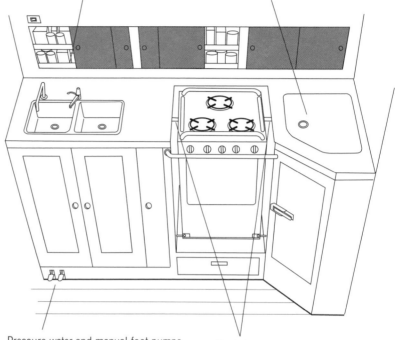

Pressure water and manual foot pumps for fresh and salt water ease your cleanup and conserve water.

Gimbals on a stove assure maximum safety while cooking underway.

NOTE: Watch small children carefully. A curious child may pull on the stove, causing pots and their contents to spill. Opening the oven door may also offset the balance.

A handy cooler for drinks cuts down use of the galley refrigerator. Barbecue downwind of the cockpit, making sure sparks don't blow into your dinghy or onto another boat.

Stoves

Most charter boats have propane stoves, although you may encounter alcohol or compressed natural gas (CNG) stoves as well. All stoves require careful operation. Propane and CNG fumes can be dangerous. Lighter than air, CNG dissipates quickly while the heavier propane fumes settle in the bilge. Ask the charter staff to demonstrate the proper use of the stove so everyone on board will understand its operation and necessary safety precautions.

Do's & Don'ts

- ▶ Do check the location of shutoff valves and solenoid switches.
- ▶ Do locate the fire extinguisher and the fire blanket, if there is one.
- ▶ Do shut off the stove fuel supply when not in use.
- ▶ Don't leave the burner and oven controls on after you turn off the fuel supply.
- ▶ Don't forget to close the tank valves when you leave the boat.

Propane Stove

Propane is efficient and easy to use but it must be treated with respect. For safety and convenience, a solenoid switch near the stove opens and closes the fuel supply at the tank. In the event of fire, turn off the solenoid. If a burner doesn't light, be sure the solenoid is on.

PROPANE STOVE OPERATION
1. Turn on the tank valve, and then the solenoid switch.
2. Strike the match or starter before turning on the burner control.
3. When you finish cooking, turn off the solenoid and then the burners.
4. Check that all stove and oven controls are off.

Alcohol Stove

Priming an alcohol stove heats the burner to make the pressurized fuel vaporize on contact and burn. Don't forget to re-prime the alcohol stove if the burner has cooled off.

ALCOHOL STOVE OPERATION
1. Pump the tank and then open the valve to allow alcohol to run into burner cup.
2. To prime the stove, close valve and ignite alcohol in burner cup.
3. When the alcohol in the cup has burned out, open valve to the burner to access fuel. Ignite the vaporizing alcohol at the burner.
4. When finished cooking, shut off valve and release pressure.

CNG Stove

OPERATION
1. Turn on the tank valve and then the solenoid, if any.
2. Strike match or starter before turning on the burner control.
3. After cooking, turn off the solenoid (if any), the burners and then the tank valve.

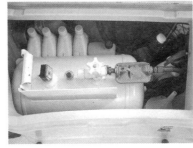

Both CNG (above) and propane (left) tanks have shutoff valves on their tanks. They should always be closed before you leave the boat or when you have finished cooking for the day. Even unlabeled, the shapes of the tanks make it possible to distinguish the fuels from one another.

Safety

Safety plays an important role in the success of your cruise. Avoid accidents by using safety gear, exercising caution around fire, protecting yourself from the sun and following other safety guidelines. Familiarize yourself thoroughly with the location of safety gear, how to use it and the quickest way out from down below. Also, make sure all crew members know how to make an emergency call on the boat's radio.

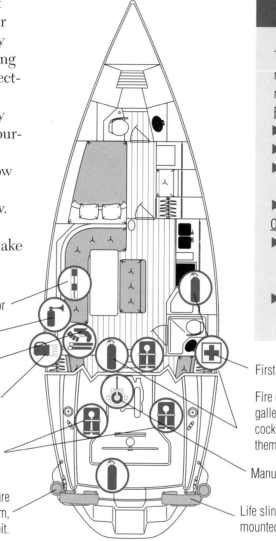

radar reflector

horn

flares

flashlight

You frequently find PFDs and harnesses in the cockpit locker or below near the companionway.

MOB pole and ring are mounted on the transom, backstay or stern pulpit.

First Aid kit

Fire extinguishers are located near the galley, the engine compartment, and the cockpit. On big boats, you'll often find them near a forward hatch as well.

Manual bilge pump

Life slings and horseshoe rings are often mounted on the transom or stern pulpit.

SAFETY EQUIPMENT CHECKLIST

The charter customer is responsible for ensuring the required gear is on board.
Before leaving the dock:
▶ Locate all fire extinguishers.
▶ Try on PFDs and harnesses.
▶ Know how to use EPIRB, flares and other safety gear.
▶ Know how to use VHF radio.
Once you're underway:
▶ Know how to use crew overboard equipment and practice recovery.
▶ Try out Lifesling, making sure to fasten the bitter end.

Sun Protection

Prolonged sun exposure causes sunburn and contributes to the development of skin cancer. Wear sunblock, broad brimmed hats and long sleeved, lightweight shirts to protect yourself. Good sunglasses protect your eyes from glare and harmful ultraviolet rays. Avoid direct sun, especially between 10 a.m. and 4 p.m. To reduce the chance of heat exhaustion or stroke, don't overexert yourself and drink plenty of water, even if you're in the shade.

Photo courtesy CYOA

Have crew try on a PFD to make sure it fits and secures properly.

Photo courtesy David Forbes

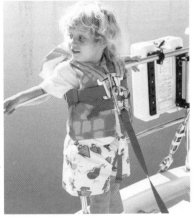

Young children should wear a PFD or harness at all times on deck, underway or at anchor.

Hand-holds and lifelines are an important part of safety. Be sure lifeline gates are closed.

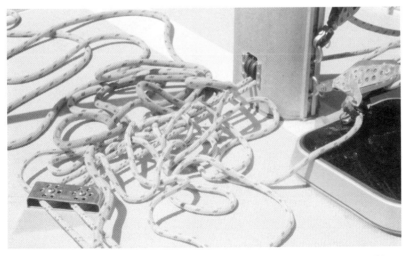

Competent sailors don't leave tangled lines. Coiled lines and good seamanship prevent emergencies!

RADIO EMERGENCIES

1. Speak slowly and clearly.
2. Make the call on Channel 16. If the emergency is life-threatening, say "Mayday, Mayday, Mayday." If the call is urgent, but not life-threatening, use "Pan, Pan, Pan." If the call is a warning, use "Securite, Securite, Securite."
3. Identify the boat with call sign and/or name three times.
4. Repeat 2 and 3 again.
5. Give your location in either latitude and longitude or bearing and distance from a known object.
6. Specify the nature of the emergency.
7. Relate details of injury or sickness with age and sex of victim.
8. Describe boat damage, if any, and seaworthiness.
9. End transmission with call sign and/or name and "over," which indicates you expect a response, or "out" which indicates you are finished.
10. Stay calm and stand by.

Do's & Don'ts

▶ Do clarify your charter company's definition of "emergency."

▶ Do try to problem solve before calling for help.

▶ Don't forget to note what radio channel or telephone number you should use to contact the charter office.

Sail Inventory

The vast majority of charter boats are sloops and your sail selection will be, in most cases, limited to main and jib. Some mains may have full-length battens which make the sail easier to control and reduce harmful flogging. You may have a larger jib for light winds and a smaller one for heavier winds. Many charter boats now come equipped with roller furling jibs which can be adjusted in size by rolling them on the luff. Likewise, you may encounter a battenless mainsail that rolls into the mast. Both of these convenient systems require correct handling. Make sure your charter staff instructs you on their proper use.

When properly furled, only the sail's protective coverings will show.

A furling line rotates a drum at the mast to roll up a mainsail.

The topping lift supports the boom when reefing and rolling up or lowering the mainsail.

An extra-long outhaul unrolls a roller furling mainsail.

Keep a slight tension on the furling line as you unroll the jib to prevent overrides on the furling drum.

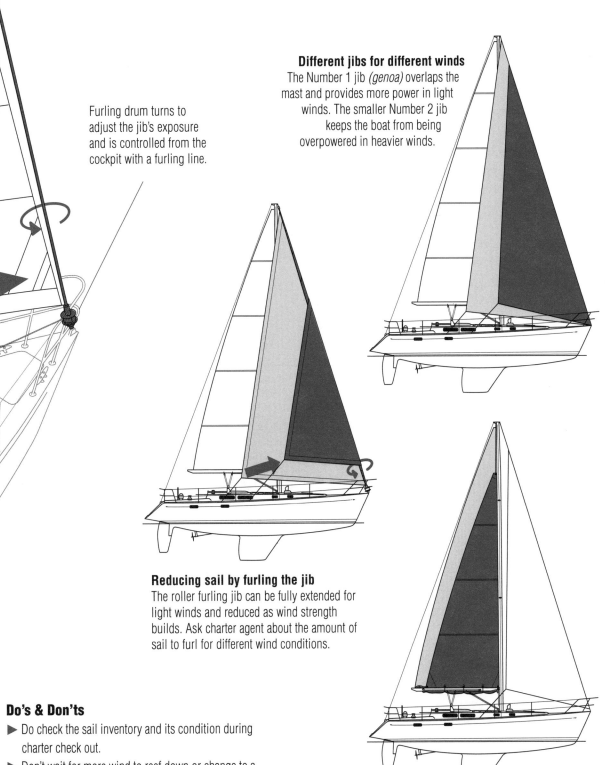

Furling drum turns to adjust the jib's exposure and is controlled from the cockpit with a furling line.

Different jibs for different winds

The Number 1 jib *(genoa)* overlaps the mast and provides more power in light winds. The smaller Number 2 jib keeps the boat from being overpowered in heavier winds.

Reducing sail by furling the jib

The roller furling jib can be fully extended for light winds and reduced as wind strength builds. Ask charter agent about the amount of sail to furl for different wind conditions.

Do's & Don'ts

▶ Do check the sail inventory and its condition during charter check out.

▶ Don't wait for more wind to reef down or change to a smaller jib. If you expect heavier winds, reduce sail early and be prepared.

▶ Do furl and unfurl a roller furling jib under control.

▶ Don't use too much pressure on the furling line as it might jeopardize the furling mechanism.

Reduce mainsail for more control

Reducing the mainsail by reefing keeps the boat more upright and comfortable in heavy winds.

Dinghy Management

Think of your dinghy like the family car or a bicycle. Run errands with it, visit other boats or go snorkeling. Before doing so, know how to tie your dinghy properly for towing, how to carry it on deck, and how to operate the outboard. Review safe boarding from the boat and the water. Remember to run the outboard at slow speed as you power through an anchorage to keep your wake at a minimum.

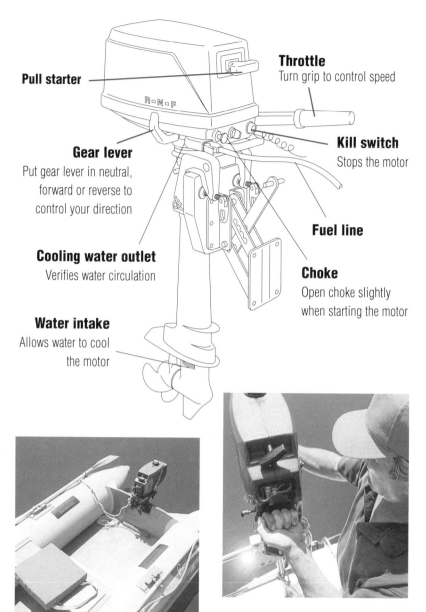

Pull starter

Throttle
Turn grip to control speed

Gear lever
Put gear lever in neutral, forward or reverse to control your direction

Kill switch
Stops the motor

Cooling water outlet
Verifies water circulation

Fuel line

Choke
Open choke slightly when starting the motor

Water intake
Allows water to cool the motor

Starting Procedure:

1. Secure tilt control lever in down position.
2. Check for adequate fuel in tank.
3. Open fuel tank vent.
4. Check that both ends of fuel line are securely attached.
5. Pump bulb firm.
6. Put gear lever in neutral.
7. Pull choke out.
8. Put throttle in start position.
9. Pull starter.
10. Check cooling water outlet.
11. Push choke in after engine starts.
12. If engine floods, push choke in, open throttle all the way and pull cord several times. Alternatively, wait several minutes and try again.

Carry PFDs and oars in the dinghy and secure the safety line to prevent losing the outboard, especially when transferring it to and from the dinghy.

The outboard is often stowed on the stern pulpit. To avoid spillage, drain extra fuel in the carburetor by disconnecting the fuel line or closing the fuel valve while the engine is still running.

DINGHY CHECKLIST

▶ Charter company policies on towing and storing the outboard vary. Clarify any questions before leaving the charter dock.
▶ Side tie the dinghy on the aft quarter when you maneuver the boat in reverse.
▶ Keep the towline/painter away from the boat's propeller, even if it's a floating polypropylene line.
▶ Remove all gear, oars, the fuel tank and the outboard when you tow.
▶ If towing with engine, tilt the engine.
▶ Double check knots when tying the dinghy.

Ventilation

In warm climates, your comfort below decks will often depend on adequate ventilation. Underway, you'll usually keep hatches and ports closed to prevent spray going below. After anchoring, open up your boat to refresh and cool the cabin.

Wind scoop is a cloth funnel suspended from the jib halyard and forestay to direct air into the forepeak.

Hatches should be latched open to permit free flow of air through the boat.

Dorade cowls permit air to enter and exit below decks.

Stern cowls ventilate the aft sections of the boat.

Ports open into the interior and can be fastened to allow circulation.

Underway, a properly designed Dorade allows the cowl to face forward for ventilation and prevent spray from going below. Face cowls aft if water enters the cabin.

VENTILATION TIPS

WHEN ANCHORED:
▶ Open all ports and hatches to increase airflow.
▶ Suspend wind scoop in forward most hatch.
▶ Position cowls on Dorade to intake and expel air.
▶ 12-volt fans draw considerable power. Monitor battery condition.

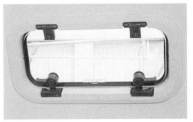

Anchored or docked, open all ports to allow fresh air into the boat. If you leave the boat unattended, close any port that might give access to valuables.

Secure ports underway to prevent spray intrusion below. Both dogs (latches) should be tightened equally.

Dodgers and Awnings

The dodger protects you from spray and, to a degree, the sun. The plastic windows should provide good visibility in all directions so you can see traffic, obstacles and sail trim. The bimini, a type of sun awning, may be used underway in some conditions. Without a plastic window overhead, though, you'll have difficulty monitoring sail trim.

Secure the folding dodger in the closed position with ties to prevent wind from accidentally opening it. Check with your charter company to see if your dodger is designed to fold.

You can snap or zipper covers over the windows for privacy or protection from UV rays when you are not underway.

Rinse the plastic windows periodically to remove salt.

Use the handles on the side of the dodger as you traverse the deck.

Frames support the dodger but aren't strong enough to be handholds unless reinforced.

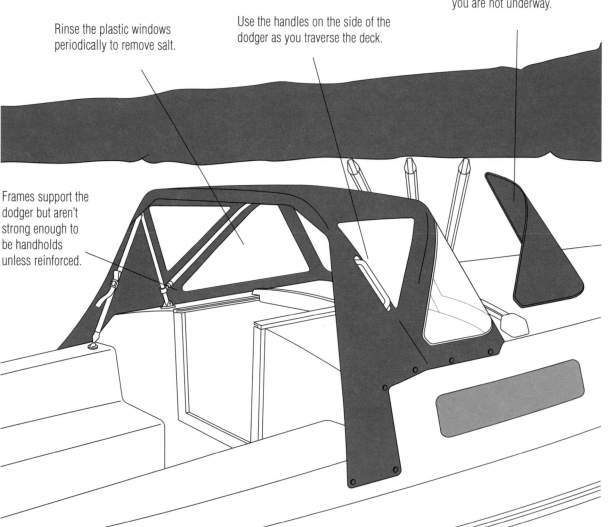

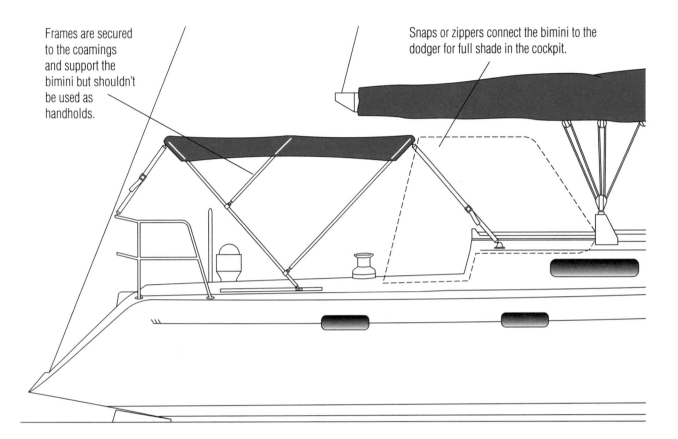

Frames are secured to the coamings and support the bimini but shouldn't be used as handholds.

Snaps or zippers connect the bimini to the dodger for full shade in the cockpit.

When not using the bimini, secure it with ties.

DODGER CHECKLIST

► Secure dodger in open or closed position, not halfway.
► Clean plastic windows for good visibility.
► Use handholds to move about on deck.
► Lower and secure folding dodger in high winds.

Do's & Don'ts

► Do use your bimini to protect crew from too much exposure to the sun.
► Do secure canvas dodger and awnings in high winds or when not in use.
► Don't use bimini or dodger if it impairs visibility.
► Don't stand or lean on the dodger.

Weather and the Sailing Environment

Before you leave the charter dock, check the weather prediction for the next few days. Local weather stations will carry up-to-date information. Rapid and/or large barometric pressure movements usually indicate major changes in the weather.

When warm, moist air cools below its dew point, fog forms. Bays and harbors can be shrouded in fog when cool water meets land-warmed air or a cold upwelling of water meets warm air as on the Northern California coast. When cold water meets a warm current, such as the Gulf Stream, fog forms at sea.

Photo courtesy Anne Gram

Ask about the local tides and currents before you leave the charter dock. Some areas of the world experience 24 foot tides twice daily, while others have virtually no tidal change at all. Note the "lean" and "wake" of a buoy to determine direction and strength of currents. Photo courtesy Anne Martin

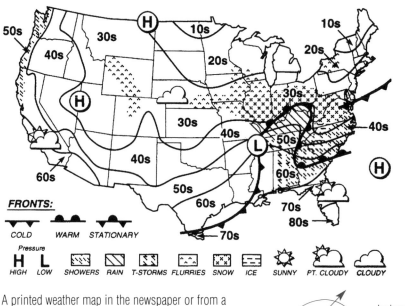

FRONTS:

COLD WARM STATIONARY

Pressure

H L   SHOWERS RAIN T-STORMS FLURRIES SNOW ICE SUNNY PT. CLOUDY CLOUDY
HIGH LOW

A printed weather map in the newspaper or from a weatherfax machine shows high ((H)) and low ((L)) pressure systems. Wind circulates clockwise around a high and counterclockwise around a low in the Northern Hemisphere, generally following the concentric lines on the map called isobars. Each isobar measures a specific level of air pressure. Tightly spaced isobars indicate a strong weather system and high winds. With this information, you can estimate wind direction and intensity.

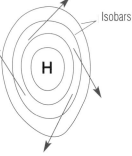

Isobars

Cold front:

Cold air replaces warm air, moving rapidly and often signaled by towering cumulus clouds. Rain, strong winds and thunderstorms can occur with cold fronts. Wind shifts clockwise as the front passes in the Northern Hemisphere.

Warm front:

Warm air replaces cold air, moving slowly (about half the speed of a cold front is the rule-of-thumb) and generally carrying lots of showery precipitation. If air is unstable, a warm front may bring thunderstorms and strong winds.

Stationary front:

When air masses of equal pressure oppose each other, the front doesn't move. Surface winds parallel the front. Weather associated with a stationary front is similar to a warm front but less intense.

Radio Weather Reports

Local weather reports for U.S. coastal waters, updated every three hours, are usually available on VHF weather channels. On multiband short wave radio, the WWV frequencies of 2500, 5000, 10000, 15000, and 20000 kHz, carry world wide emergency weather information before and after the hourly time signal. These reports include the latitude and longitude positions for dense fog, icebergs and hurricanes.

High cirrus clouds (Mares' Tails) usually indicate an approaching warm front with rain and wind changes in the next 48 hours. The cloud cover will become lower and denser.

Rapidly moving black clouds indicate squalls. The clouds appear to be in long rows or lines. Squalls, usually of short duration, may have rain, strong winds and a change of direction, so respond quickly with immediate action.

Stock Newport photo

HURRICANE SEASONS

Location	Months
Caribbean/East Coast	June - November
South Pacific	December-April
West Coast	June - November

East Coast

East Coast weather patterns change constantly as the continental land mass reconfigures passing weather fronts. Cool Canadian highs mix with warm, moist air from the south to create towering cumulus clouds which can become thunderstorms in the warmer months. Cold fronts move unpredictably but are usually followed by puffy and shifty northwesterlies. Late summer fog is common along New England's shores, particularly in the hot months of July and August.

West Coast

West Coast weather forms over the Pacific Ocean. Winter storms track across the ocean and bring rain. From April through October, a huge, relatively stationary offshore high pressure system, called the Pacific High, provides sunny weather and steady westerly breezes. Coastal areas experience regular sea breezes as the land heats up and the air flows from the sea to the land. Those areas adjacent to warm inland valleys frequently experience very strong afternoon winds and fog during the summer. Strong westerlies sometimes counter tidal currents and create unusually short and choppy waves such as can be found on San Francisco Bay. Winter cold fronts over the desert cause strong easterlies, called Santa Anas, which can extend many miles offshore in Southern California.

Island Weather

In the tropics, where large land masses are scarce, trade winds predominate. Usually lighter in the morning, these winds peak at around 20 knots in the evening. Puffy, flat-bottomed clouds scud across the brilliant blue sky. Close to the equator, the Inter Tropical Convergence Zone features light winds, squalls, and warm, overcast weather. The Caribbean's easterly Christmas winds may bring some wind velocities up to 30 knots. Spring features lighter breezes and dry weather.

Passage Planning

"So much to see, so little time!" Resist the temptation to do too much. Use your chart to calculate the distances between the places you want to visit. At an average of five or six knots, how far can you sail in a day? Will you be sailing to weather or downwind? Most charter companies require you to reach your anchorage by mid-afternoon, so factor that into your departure time. Explore your recreational and sight-seeing options for each destination.

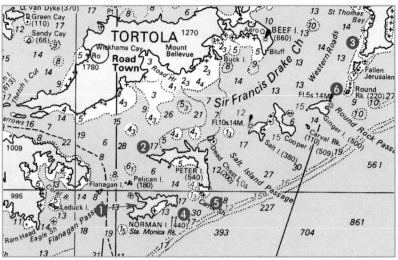

charts for page 36-37 reproduced from Imray-Iolaire chart A 231 by permission of Imray Laurie Norie and Wilson Ltd

---

PASSAGE PLANNING

▶ Select a passage that's comfortable for everyone. Reaching is more comfortable than beating and protected waters offer less waves and swells.

▶ Go with the current whenever possible.

▶ Check for adequate depth along the entire route.

▶ Estimate time and distance for your passage. Allow for extra time and distance if tacking to a windward destination as it increases your distance by approximately 1/3.

▶ Estimate fuel consumption if planning a long passage under power to ensure you'll have sufficient fuel. Check the boat book or ask the charter agent for the rate (gallons per hour), otherwise use one gallon per hour.

In planning a passage from the Bight on Norman Island to The Baths on Virgin Gorda, you can choose the more protected route through the Sir Francis Drake Channel or the outside passage through open seas and swells. Both cover about 16 to 18 nautical miles and include beating to windward in easterly winds. At an average speed of 6 knots (nautical miles per hour), the trip takes about 3 hours (18nm/6kts = 3hrs). The Sir Francis Drake Channel passage offers smoother waters with several harbors of refuge. Leave the Bight **1** on a reach to pass the western tip of Peter Island **2** and then tack up the Channel to The Baths **3**. The outside passage passes Norman **4** and Peter **5** Islands to the south on a beat to Round Rock Passage **6**. With good timing, a favorable 1 knot tidal current can help you through the Passage, finishing on a reach to The Baths **3**.

Calculating Time

If you assume an average speed of 6 knots and measure the distance on the chart as 12 miles, it would take 2 hours

$$T = \frac{D}{S} = \frac{12\,nm}{6\,knots} \qquad T = \textbf{2 hours}$$

Calculating Fuel Consumption

F (Fuel) = **R** (rate of consumption) x **T** (time)

or $\mathbf{F} = \dfrac{\mathbf{R} \times \mathbf{D}}{\mathbf{S}}$

F = 0.75 gal/hr x 60 nm ÷ 6 knots

F = 7.5 gallons

Do's & Don'ts

▶ Do encourage all of your crew to participate in passage planning.

▶ Do have more than one plan for each day.

▶ Don't forget to plan extra time in case of bad weather or if you want to stay longer at an appealing location.

▶ Do leave a passage itinerary with the charter office, and check in with them if your plans change.

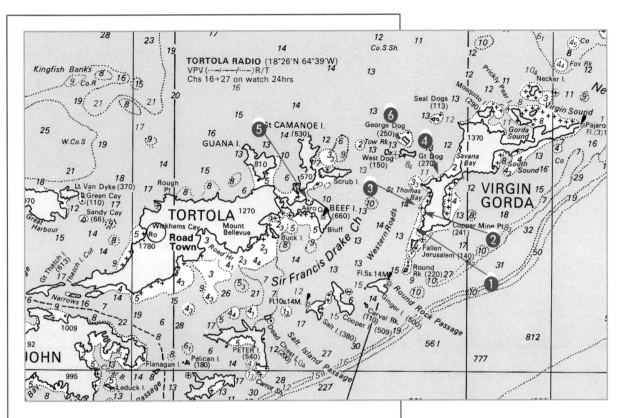

The Baths ❶ Anchoring here is restricted to daylight hours. The rocky bottom requires careful selection of anchoring location. Many mooring buoys have been placed at the Baths. The area is protected in easterlies, but swell is common, so be careful landing your dinghy on the beach.

Virgin Gorda Yacht Harbor ❷ You must sail almost to Colison Point in order to make the marked entrance channel to the yacht harbor.

St. Thomas Bay ❸ The best anchorage is in the northeastern corner, under Colison Point. A northwest ground swell can come in at night and the wind eddies may swing you around, so consider two anchors or a Bahamian moor. Note the coral heads on the island shelf.

Little Dix Bay ❹ On the west side of Virgin Gorda and open to the northwest, Little Dix Bay is around the point from the yacht harbor and may be crowded. From here, you have an easy sail to The Baths or to Gorda Sound farther north.

Trellis Bay ❺ This is a convenient anchorage on the Sir Frances Drake Channel opposite Round Rock Passage on Beef Island. If you are behind schedule or need a rest, Trellis Bay offers a large, protected anchorage in all conditions with a sandy bottom for easy anchoring and retrieval. Do not anchor within 200 feet of the western shore, which is the passage for ferries and freighters. Also avoid the small reef in the middle of the bay and the phone cable, which is buoyed.

George Dog ❻ A great day anchorage with excellent snorkeling. The rocky bottom may challenge your anchoring skills, but it's close to Gorda Sound and Beef Island.

Night Sailing

Most charter companies require that you anchor before sunset. Unforeseen circumstances may find you underway after dark, however. If the entrance to a harbor is unlighted or obstructed, good seamanship calls for standing off for the night. In shallow waters, anchor with an anchor light and avoid ship channels. Heave-to if the water's too deep and you have searoom to leeward. An unobstructed, well-lighted harbor may be entered by an experienced skipper and crew using a chart and depth sounder and everyone on watch.

Always plan for alternative anchorages. During busy seasons, your original choice may be crowded. If weather patterns change, you may find yourself exposed to wind and seas. Tidal range, current and the type of holding ground may require you to anchor in an alternate location or use two anchors instead of one. Some popular anchorages are only usable during the day because of changing evening winds and swell patterns.

Leaving the Dock

You will have a hard time pushing a larger boat away from the dock. Instead, use the boat's spring lines for leverage. Plan your departure beforehand and make sure everyone on board knows what's going to happen and what to do. Crew members should be prepared with fenders in hand to fend off obstacles or other boats, as necessary. Go slowly and if things aren't working, stop and start over again.

Do's & Don'ts

▶ Don't leave the dock without snugging the dinghy to the outside (outboard) aft quarter. Once in clear water, the dinghy can be towed off the stern.

▶ Do rig your spring lines at either the bow or stern, not amidships, when using them to spring the boat away from the dock.

▶ Do cast off docklines in order of least tensioned first and the doubled up working spring line last.

▶ Do account for the effect of prop walk on your boat's movement.

Doubling the spring line allows you to release it from aboard the boat. Pass it around the dock cleat and back to the boat. Bring the line in quickly to prevent fouling the propeller.

Upwind Departure

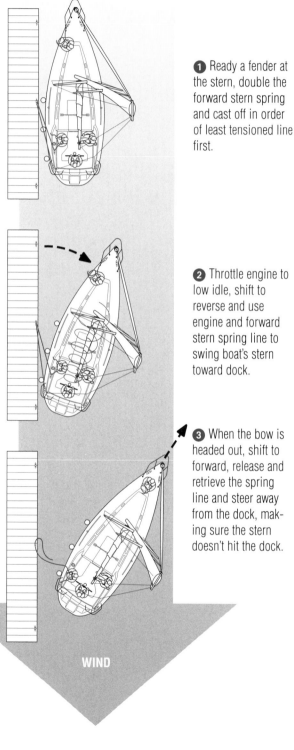

1 Ready a fender at the stern, double the forward stern spring and cast off in order of least tensioned line first.

2 Throttle engine to low idle, shift to reverse and use engine and forward stern spring line to swing boat's stern toward dock.

3 When the bow is headed out, shift to forward, release and retrieve the spring line and steer away from the dock, making sure the stern doesn't hit the dock.

WIND

Downwind Departure

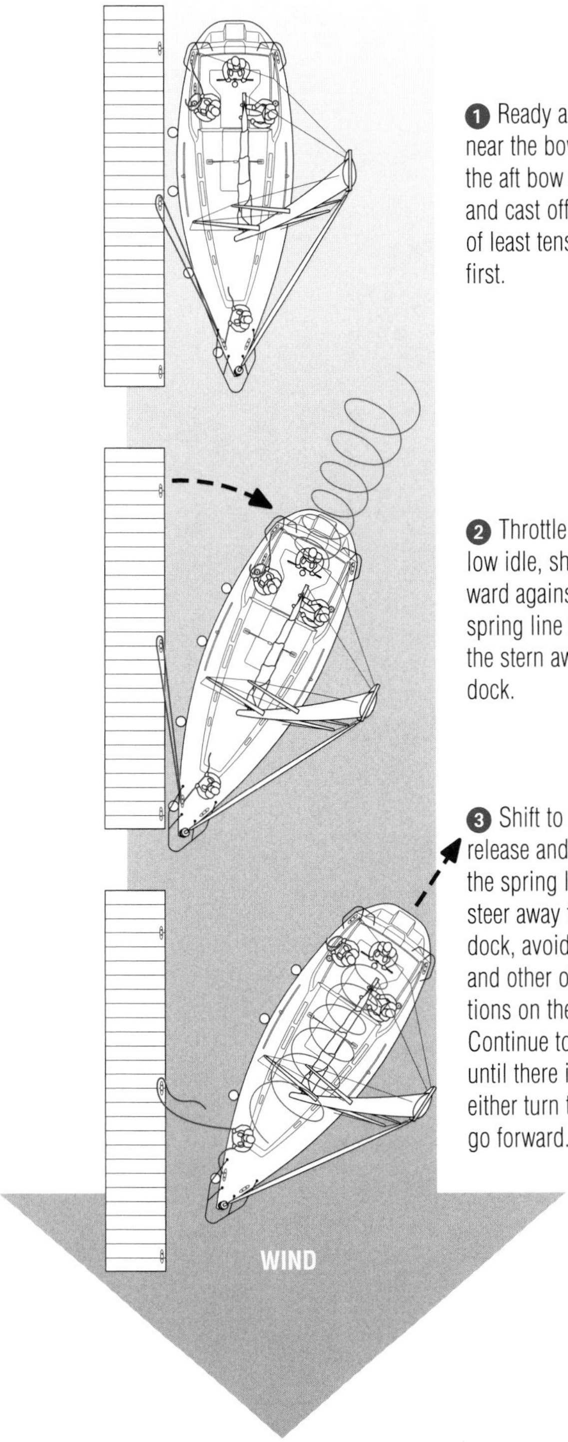

1 Ready a fender near the bow, double the aft bow spring and cast off, in order of least tensioned line first.

2 Throttle engine to low idle, shift to forward against the spring line to swing the stern away from dock.

3 Shift to reverse, release and retrieve the spring line and steer away from the dock, avoiding pilings and other obstructions on the dock. Continue to reverse until there is room to either turn the boat or go forward.

WIND

Crosswind Departure

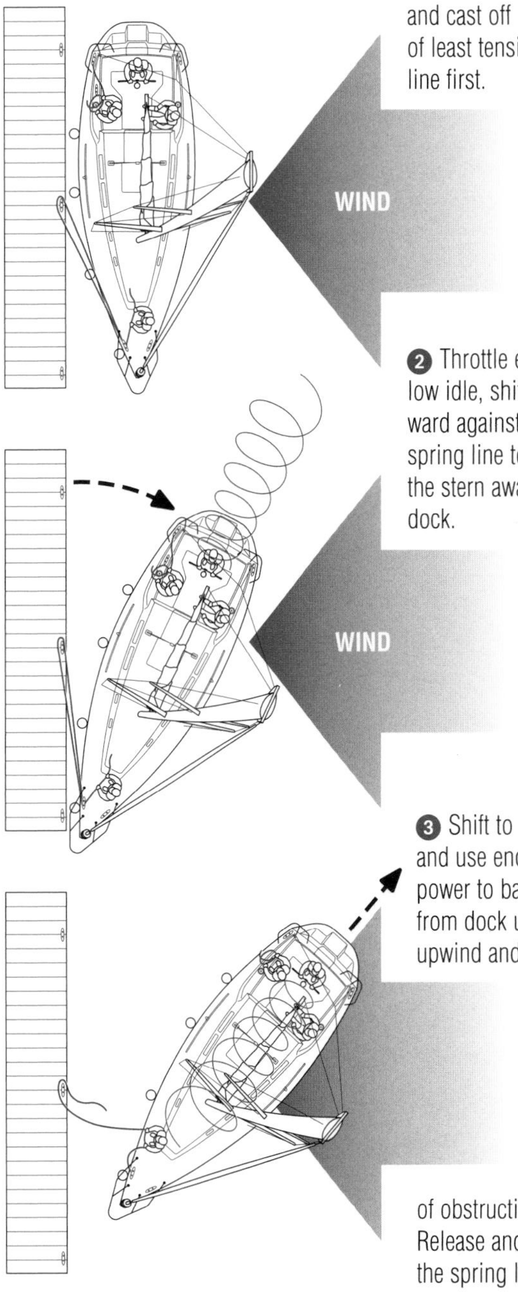

1 Ready a fender near the bow, double the aft bow spring and cast off in order of least tensioned line first.

WIND

2 Throttle engine to low idle, shift to forward against the spring line to swing the stern away from dock.

WIND

3 Shift to reverse and use enough power to back away from dock until upwind and clear

of obstructions. Release and retrieve the spring line. Continue backing away until you're free to go forward.

Maneuvering under Power

A boat's windage varies with the size and shape of the topsides. Windage increases with more wind and as the wind moves to the beam. Learn how windage influences your boat and practice compensating for it. Under power, you feel the effects of windage increase as you slow down and the boat becomes more difficult to maneuver.

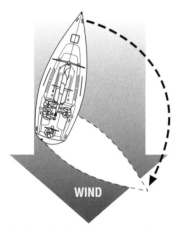

The bow "falls off" and turns downwind from windage. Steer into the wind to avoid "falling off."

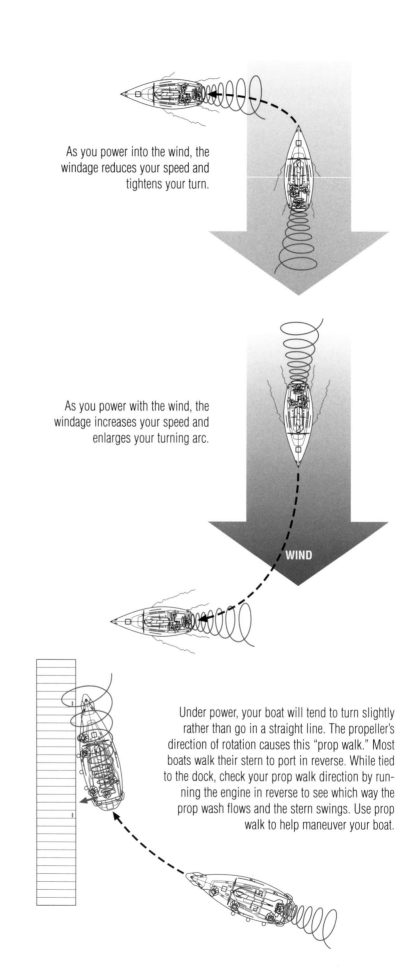

As you power into the wind, the windage reduces your speed and tightens your turn.

As you power with the wind, the windage increases your speed and enlarges your turning arc.

Under power, your boat will tend to turn slightly rather than go in a straight line. The propeller's direction of rotation causes this "prop walk." Most boats walk their stern to port in reverse. While tied to the dock, check your prop walk direction by running the engine in reverse to see which way the prop wash flows and the stern swings. Use prop walk to help maneuver your boat.

STOPPING AND SHIFTING

- ▶ Shift gears only at idle by reducing the throttle.
- ▶ Shift into reverse to brake the forward motion of the boat. Increase throttle to hasten your stop.
- ▶ Windage changes the distance required for stopping.

Making a Tight Turn

Turning in tight spaces, such as between moored boats or in a narrow marina fairway, requires a technique called "backing and filling." Prop walk becomes an asset in these situations. If your boat kicks its stern to port in reverse, you'll back and fill by turning the boat clockwise (bow to starboard). If the stern kicks to starboard, make the turn counterclockwise. Boats will handle differently due to differences in underwater profile, propeller position, displacement and windage. Remember: Lines can be used to maneuver a boat in tight quarters. This is called *warping*.

Do's & Don'ts

▶ Do use the prop walk to help turn the boat.

▶ Don't forget water must be flowing past the rudder for it to have any effect. The effect is faster in forward gear than in reverse.

▶ Do test forward and reverse gears of the transmission before you need them.

▶ Do check out the handling characteristics of your boat before entering close quarters.

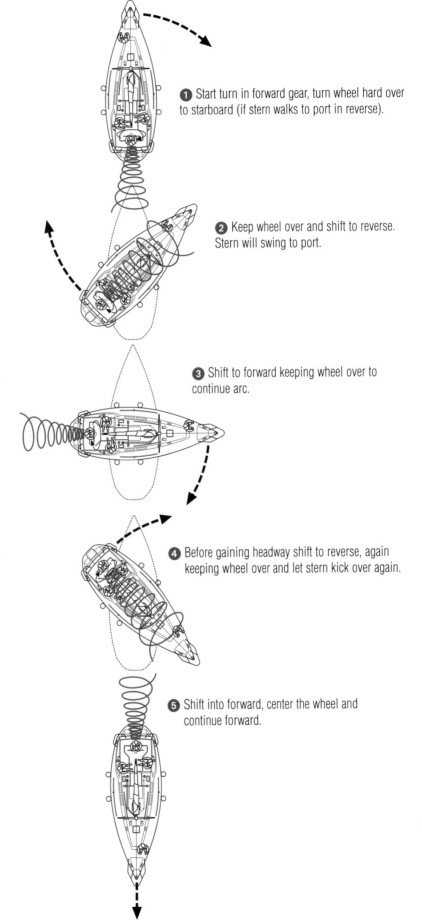

❶ Start turn in forward gear, turn wheel hard over to starboard (if stern walks to port in reverse).

❷ Keep wheel over and shift to reverse. Stern will swing to port.

❸ Shift to forward keeping wheel over to continue arc.

❹ Before gaining headway shift to reverse, again keeping wheel over and let stern kick over again.

❺ Shift into forward, center the wheel and continue forward.

Docking

Docking a larger boat requires the same skills you learned on small boats. In addition, you'll use midship spring lines for more control and you'll have to pay more attention to the boat's inertia and windage. If you have a choice, approach the dock with the bow into the wind to help slow your forward momentum. Use prop walk to bring the boat alongside the dock whenever possible.

DOCKING CHECKLIST

▶ Check all lines are clear of the propeller.

▶ Secure the dinghy on the outboard aft quarter.

▶ Place fenders at dock level and fasten them to stanchions with a round turn and two half-hitches.

Upwind Docking

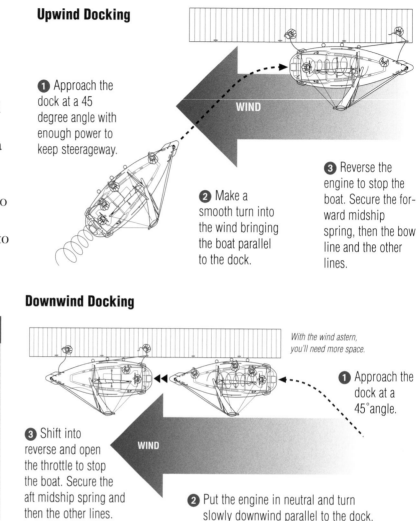

❶ Approach the dock at a 45 degree angle with enough power to keep steerageway.

❷ Make a smooth turn into the wind bringing the boat parallel to the dock.

❸ Reverse the engine to stop the boat. Secure the forward midship spring, then the bow line and the other lines.

Downwind Docking

With the wind astern, you'll need more space.

❸ Shift into reverse and open the throttle to stop the boat. Secure the aft midship spring and then the other lines.

❷ Put the engine in neutral and turn slowly downwind parallel to the dock.

❶ Approach the dock at a 45°angle.

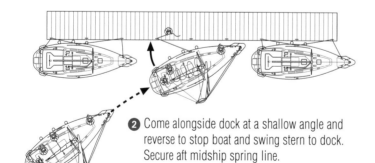

❷ Come alongside dock at a shallow angle and reverse to stop boat and swing stern to dock. Secure aft midship spring line.

Close Quarters Docking

Motor slowly past your desired location to check the wind, current and the direction of approach. Return with lines prepared. If you don't like the space situation or it exceeds your comfort zone, ask the dockmaster for another location.

❶ Approach slowly with enough power for steerageway.

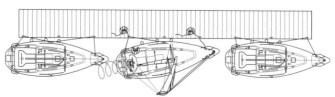

❸ Shift to forward and turn wheel away from dock to bring the boat alongside the dock and hold it in position while the other lines are made fast.

Crosswind Docking (leeward side)

Approaching the leeward side of the dock, windage will work against you.

1 At low speed, turn the boat directly into the wind until you are about a half boat length from the dock.

2 Make a tight turn to bring the boat parallel to the dock.

WIND

3 Reverse the engine to stop and secure the aft midship spring. Shift to forward and turn the wheel to hold the boat against the dock while the crew secures the other lines.

Do's & Don'ts

▶ Do step onto the dock from the shrouds with docklines in hand.

▶ Don't be afraid to abandon a docking that's not working and try again.

▶ Do use midship spring lines to bring boat alongside dock and hold it in position.

Crosswind Docking (windward side)

Approaching the windward side of the dock, the boat's windage will push you against the dock.

1 Approach the dock at an angle.

2 When half a boat length away, turn the boat almost parallel to the dock but with the bow cocked toward the wind.

3 Reverse the engine to stop the boat as it drifts into the dock. Secure the aft midship spring and then the other lines.

WIND

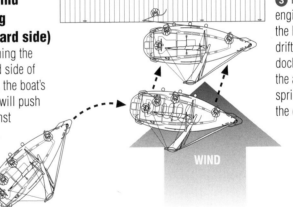

Securing the Boat

Led from midships, the aft spring line prevents forward motion and the forward spring line prevents motion aft. When securing the boat to a fixed dock in tidal waters, allow for the water level's rise and fall by leading the stern line to the outboard quarter.

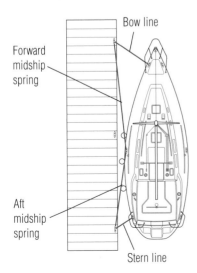

Bow line

Forward midship spring

Aft midship spring

Stern line

Having secured fenders, and docklines in hand, this crew stands by the shrouds ready to step onto the dock.

Motorsailing

There will be times when you may need or want to motorsail. Keep the sail properly trimmed to the apparent wind and avoid heading directly upwind. Flogging the main could cause damage for which a charter company can hold you responsible. Putting in a reef will flatten the sail and make trimming easier. Heeling may affect engine operation, so check your oil pressure and temperature gauges regularly.

When motorsailing in International waters, Navigation Rule 25(e) requires an inverted black cone. The same applies for Inland waters except for boats less than 12 meters (39.4 feet).

Do's & Don'ts

► Do trim your sails to the wind when you motorsail.
► Don't forget the apparent wind goes forward when you motor.
► Do keep the boat upright when you motorsail.
► Don't flog the mainsail by motorsailing directly into the wind.
► Do remember you are a powerboat under the navigation rules.

When motorsailing, especially in light winds, your forward motion will draw the apparent wind toward the bow. Keep your sails trimmed to the wind as indicated by the masthead fly or the telltales.

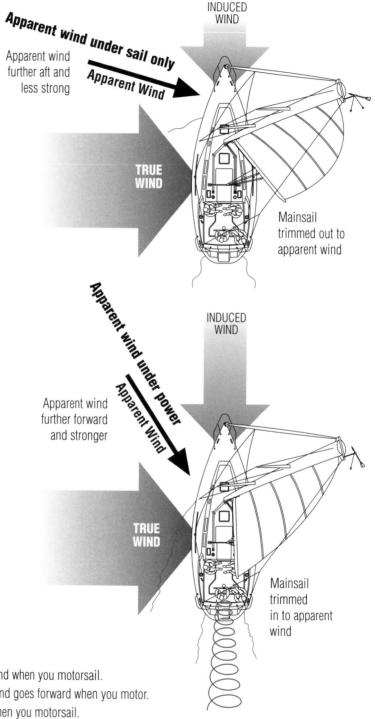

Big Boat Crewing

Crewing on a larger boat demands coordination and teamwork, not only between the helmsman and crew but also among the crew themselves. Where brute strength might suffice on a smaller boat, you'll need to focus instead on anticipation, timing and execution. Communication, especially in advance of maneuvers, is the cornerstone of success.

Commonly agreed upon hand signals are useful in situations where it's hard to be heard over the wind or other noises. Here are some typical signals:

When raising or lowering sails: thumbs up means go higher,

thumbs down means keep lowering,

clenched fist means stop.

higher

lower

stop

let out

trim

stop

When trimming sails: pointing in the direction of the sail means let it out; twirling your index finger clockwise means trim the sheet; a clenched fist means stop.

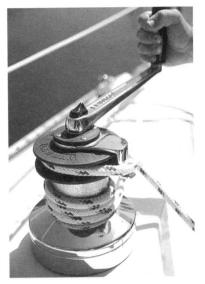

Self-tailing winches have built-in jaws on top of the winch drum which let one person grind and tail at the same time.

A winch holds a line with friction. As the load of the sail increases, add more wraps to the winch drum for greater holding power.

A locking lever on a winch handle keeps it attached to the winch drum and helps prevent losing the handle overboard.

Do's & Don'ts

▶ Do have the helmsman hold the bow close to the wind to luff the jib after a tack so the crew can grind in the sail under reduced load.

▶ Do talk over sailing maneuvers beforehand so that everyone knows what's going to happen.

▶ Don't put yourself or your crew into dangerous positions or attempt maneuvers that require a greater skill level.

▶ At least one member of the crew should always be responsible for looking under the jib to leeward for obstructions or other boats.

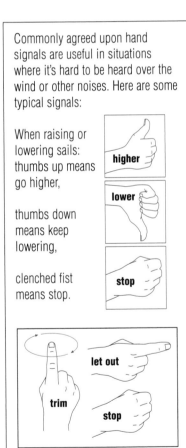

Downwind Cruising

When sailing long distances, comfort becomes important. If your destination is downwind, you might put your boat on a run, but you'll roll and pitch in moderate sea conditions. The mainsail will blanket the jib, reducing the sail's pull and creating a hazard as the jib sheets swing back and forth across the foredeck. You also risk sailing by the lee and jibing the mainsail accidentally. By heading up to a broad reach, you'll sail safer and in more comfort.

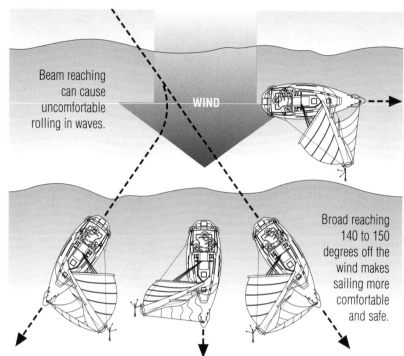

Beam reaching can cause uncomfortable rolling in waves.

WIND

Broad reaching 140 to 150 degrees off the wind makes sailing more comfortable and safe.

Running can cause uncomfortable rolling and pitching, and an accidental jibe.

A whisker pole holds the jib to windward in order to catch more wind. Fasten the inboard end of the pole to the mast and lead the jib sheet through the outboard end.

NOTE: For more advanced downwind sailing techniques, refer to US SAILING's *Passage Making.*

Steering Downwind

Lead the jib sheet to a block forward of the fairlead and outside the shrouds on the rail to loosen the foot and tighten the upper leech.

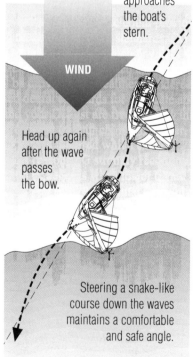

Head off slightly as the wave approaches the boat's stern.

WIND

Head up again after the wave passes the bow.

Steering a snake-like course down the waves maintains a comfortable and safe angle.

Sailing Downwind

The mainsail. Running square before the wind, the main should be strongly vanged to keep the boom down. This reduces chafe against the shrouds and spreaders which is otherwise inevitable unless you oversheet hopelessly. On a long run, particularly in an awkward sea, a boom preventer should also be rigged. This is simply a line secured to the boom end and led forward to a turning block on the foredeck. From here, it comes back to the cockpit where it is brought to a spare winch and cleated tight. If there is no winch, ease the mainsheet off, harden the preventer up as much as you can by hand, cleat the preventer, then trim the mainsheet back against it. Be sure to cleat the preventer so that it can be released under heavy load.

A boom with a preventer should be held more or less rigid. This not only saves you from the effects of an accidental jibe, it makes you far less likely to jibe in the first place. A preventer is also extremely useful in light airs to stop the boom from slapping and banging about with each roll of the boat.

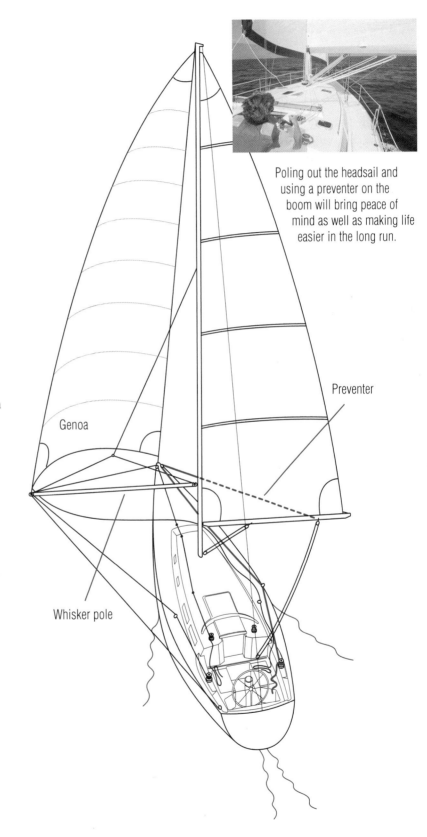

Poling out the headsail and using a preventer on the boom will bring peace of mind as well as making life easier in the long run.

Preventer

Genoa

Whisker pole

Depowering Sails

Winds vary in direction and strength during the day. If steering becomes difficult due to weather helm or you are heeling uncomfortably, depower the sails to keep the boat more upright. There are several ways to depower, and you may eventually have to reef if the wind continues to rise.

Depower with the Mainsheet
Ease the mainsheet so the boom rises and twists off the top of the sail.

Top of sail twists away from the wind, reducing power

Ease the mainsheet

Depower for Stronger Winds
Flatten the sail shape by tightening the outhaul and the cunningham. The luff of the main and the jib can also be adjusted by tightening the halyard.

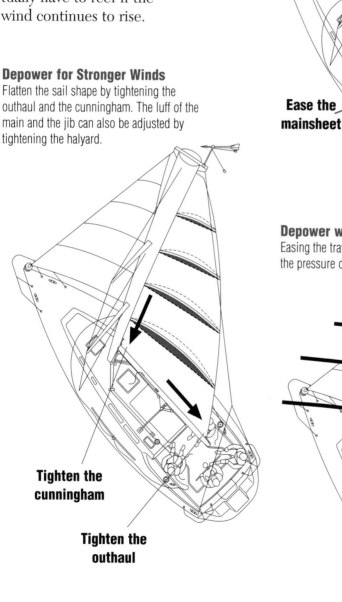

Tighten the cunningham

Tighten the outhaul

Depower with the Traveler
Easing the traveler to leeward lessens the pressure on the entire sail.

Entire sail rotates away from the wind, reducing power

Ease the traveler

Depower the Jib

Move the jib fairlead aft to twist the top of the sail to leeward. To move the lead, slide the block aft on the windward side and secure it, tack and adjust the block on the other side, then tack back. If the jib is roller furling, you can roll it up, move the block and then unroll it. Check to see if the top of the sail has depowered. If not, repeat the maneuver and slide the lead farther aft.

Feathering Sails

Other techniques will depower the sails as well. For example, when sailing upwind and a strong puff hits, you can steer the boat slightly into the No-Go Zone, which will cause the forward edge of the sails to luff and the boat to straighten up. Then steer away from the wind until the sails stop luffing and the boat picks up speed again. Repeat this maneuver, called *feathering*, to reduce heeling and weather helm.

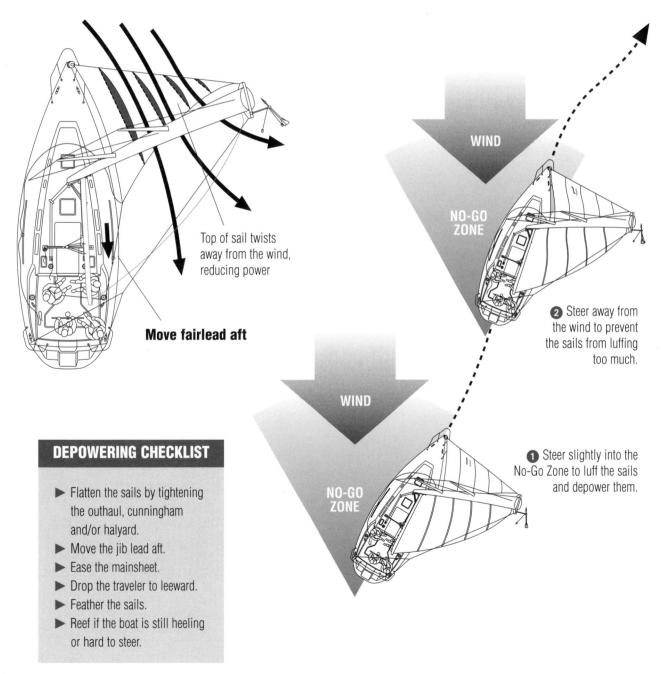

Top of sail twists away from the wind, reducing power

Move fairlead aft

WIND

NO-GO ZONE

❷ Steer away from the wind to prevent the sails from luffing too much.

WIND

NO-GO ZONE

❶ Steer slightly into the No-Go Zone to luff the sails and depower them.

DEPOWERING CHECKLIST

► Flatten the sails by tightening the outhaul, cunningham and/or halyard.
► Move the jib lead aft.
► Ease the mainsheet.
► Drop the traveler to leeward.
► Feather the sails.
► Reef if the boat is still heeling or hard to steer.

Shortening Sail

Heavy winds and seas usually require shortening sail for both safety and comfort. Reducing your exposure to the wind will put less strain on the boat and its equipment. At the same time, you want enough sail up to keep the boat moving and maintain good steering. Think of shortening sail as finding the right balance between the boat and the weather. Most importantly, reef your sails before you become overpowered, not afterwards.

Changing Headsails

1 If possible, head off the wind so the mainsail will blanket the jib. Attach the new jib's tack to the bow fitting and connect the luff to the headstay.

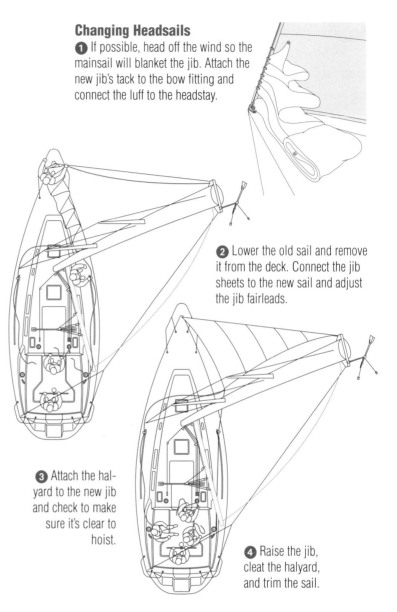

2 Lower the old sail and remove it from the deck. Connect the jib sheets to the new sail and adjust the jib fairleads.

3 Attach the halyard to the new jib and check to make sure it's clear to hoist.

4 Raise the jib, cleat the halyard, and trim the sail.

With a roller furling jib, it's easy to shorten sail by furling the jib on the headstay. Roll up the sail until you've got a comfortable heeling angle. Check with the charter agent if there is a preferred amount of sail to furl.

Too much heel creates severe weather helm and makes steering difficult.

Don't forget to move the jib fairlead forward to maintain the proper trim angle for the jib sheet.

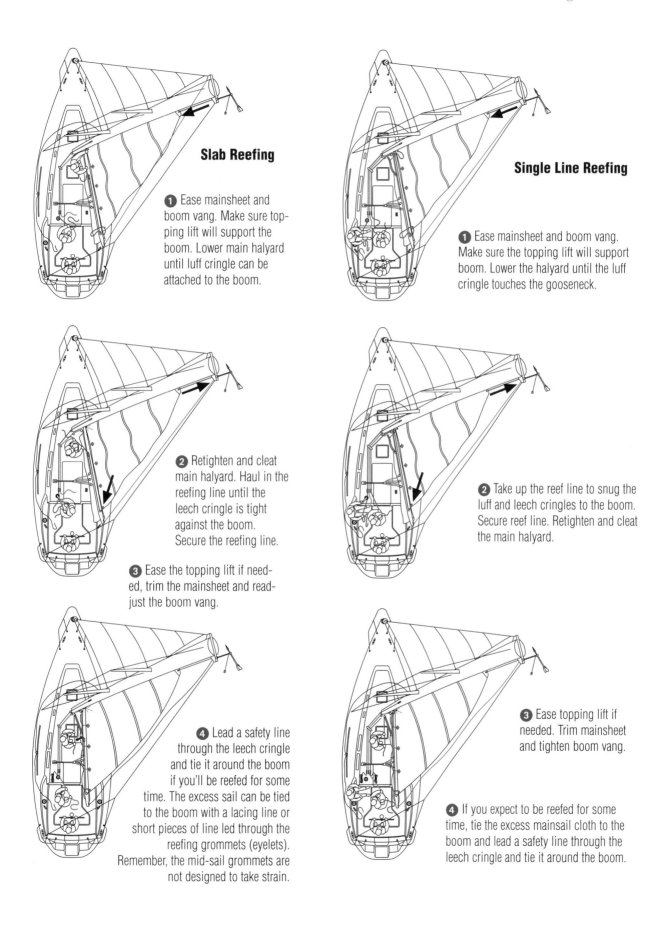

Slab Reefing

1 Ease mainsheet and boom vang. Make sure topping lift will support the boom. Lower main halyard until luff cringle can be attached to the boom.

2 Retighten and cleat main halyard. Haul in the reefing line until the leech cringle is tight against the boom. Secure the reefing line.

3 Ease the topping lift if needed, trim the mainsheet and readjust the boom vang.

4 Lead a safety line through the leech cringle and tie it around the boom if you'll be reefed for some time. The excess sail can be tied to the boom with a lacing line or short pieces of line led through the reefing grommets (eyelets). Remember, the mid-sail grommets are not designed to take strain.

Single Line Reefing

1 Ease mainsheet and boom vang. Make sure the topping lift will support boom. Lower the halyard until the luff cringle touches the gooseneck.

2 Take up the reef line to snug the luff and leech cringles to the boom. Secure reef line. Retighten and cleat the main halyard.

3 Ease topping lift if needed. Trim mainsheet and tighten boom vang.

4 If you expect to be reefed for some time, tie the excess mainsail cloth to the boom and lead a safety line through the leech cringle and tie it around the boom.

Anchoring

On a typical cruise you may anchor two or three times a day to take advantage of different opportunities. Master the techniques and skills of anchoring thoroughly so you can enjoy your cruising. Success depends on preparation, preplanning, and practice. Learn how to handle the different scenarios.

ANCHORING CHECKLIST

▶ Compare the anchorage with your chart.

▶ Determine the prevailing wind and current for the duration of your stay.

▶ Select your spot and brief the crew on your anchoring plan.

▶ Anchor in the same configuration as your neighbors so all boats swing alike.

▶ Secure the bitter end of your anchor rode before you lower the anchor.

▶ Calculate your rode length by adding your boat's freeboard to the tidal range and water depth and multiplying that figure by the desired ratio, usually 4:1 to 7:1.

▶ If anchorage is not crowded you will be most comfortable with a 7:1 ratio for a chain and line rode. Typical scope for an all chain rode is 4:1.

▶ Boats will swing in smaller arcs when anchored with an all-chain rode.

▶ Boats will swing in wider arcs when using rope rather than all-chain rode.

❶ Paradise Cove is protected from the southerly and prevailing westerly winds with little current. Beware of rocks on the shoreline.

❷ Tide rips in front of the entrance to Belvedere Cove, reaching speeds of 6 knots, require a cautious approach.

❸ Mud bottom and excellent protection from all winds, but has limited depth.

❹ Protected cove with a 10 foot, soft bottom, is good in all weather except a northeasterly.

Boats with lots of windage react more to wind direction when anchored.

Boats with deep underbodies sometimes react more to the current than to wind direction when anchored.

Your boat will rotate on its anchor with wind and current changes, so make sure your swing radius will keep you clear of all obstructions.

Anchoring under Power

Anchoring under power gives you more control of the boat than anchoring under sail. You must, however, keep all lines away from the propeller to avoid a wrap.

Review hand signals beforehand so the skipper and crew know what each signal means.

To steer to port, raise left arm with hand pointing to port.

To steer to starboard, raise the right arm with hand pointing to starboard.

To move straight ahead, raise arm and motion forward.

To indicate stop, raise arm with closed fist.

To indicate reverse, raise arm with palm facing aft.

② Shift from forward to reverse to stop the boat, and lower the anchor until it touches bottom.

① After checking the depth, approach the chosen anchor spot upwind or up current, whichever is stronger.

③ Drift or back slowly downwind or down current, letting out anchor rode until you have enough scope to set the anchor.

④ Snub the rode and reverse slowly until the rode becomes taut and the anchor is holding. While in reverse, feel the rode for chatter to make sure the anchor is set. If space permits, pay out rode to the optimum scope.

Do's & Don'ts

▶ Do furl your sails before anchoring to improve visibility.

▶ Don't forget to side tie your dinghy before starting anchoring maneuver.

▶ Do use 3-strand nylon for a rope rode, which absorbs shock loads.

▶ Don't drop the anchor and rode in a heap. Lower the anchor first and feed out the rode as you back off.

▶ Do keep track of how much rode you let out.

▶ Do remember that arriving vessels must respect the rights of vessels already anchored.

Bow and Stern Anchoring

Set fore and aft anchors in areas where there is little swinging room and little chance for wind or current on the beam, causing anchors to drag.

1 Set bow anchor as described previously and into the current. Prepare the second anchor.

2 Drift back with current or waves, paying out the original length of the bow rode again.

3 Lower the second anchor over the stern until it touches bottom.

4 Motor forward slowly, paying out stern rode and taking up bow rode until you have enough scope to set the anchor. Make the stern rode fast, continue forward slowly to set stern anchor.

5 Pay out additional stern rode to reach the equidistant position. Note, some anchors - plow and Bruce - may take more distance to set than a Danforth.

Anchoring with Two Bow Anchors

Certain conditions require two anchors to reduce swing and for extra holding power, usually separated by 60 to 90°. Use two bow anchors when nearby boats are anchored that way or when you anticipate strong and/or shifting winds.

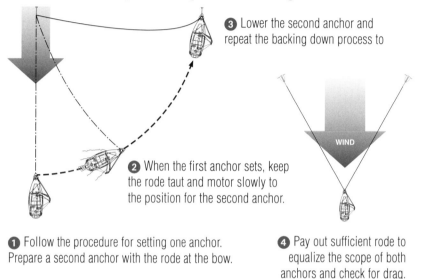

3 Lower the second anchor and repeat the backing down process to

2 When the first anchor sets, keep the rode taut and motor slowly to the position for the second anchor.

1 Follow the procedure for setting one anchor. Prepare a second anchor with the rode at the bow.

4 Pay out sufficient rode to equalize the scope of both anchors and check for drag.

Bahamian Anchoring

In areas of extreme current, set two anchors off the bow so they parallel the water's flow. When the current reverses, the load will shift from one anchor to the other and you'll minimize your swing while keeping the bow into the current. If your rode tangles around the keel as the boat rotates, pay out enough slack to let it sink under the keel and clear itself.

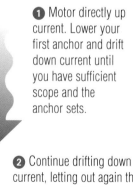

1 Motor directly up current. Lower your first anchor and drift down current until you have sufficient scope and the anchor sets.

2 Continue drifting down current, letting out again the same amount of rode as you originally set.

3 Lower your second anchor over the bow.

4 Return up current, taking in the rode from the first anchor and letting out the rode on the second anchor. Guard against fouling the rode in the prop. Set the second anchor. Recheck your bearings after the tide changes.

Setting a Second Anchor with the Dinghy

Make fast the bitter end of the second anchor rode. Put the anchor and a few feet of rode in the dinghy and row or motor while a crew member on the boat pays out the rode. When the rode of the second anchor equals that of the first, lower the anchor. Tie off the rode on the bow of the boat and back down to set the second anchor.

Another technique is as follows: Secure the bitter end of the anchor rode aboard your boat and load the anchor and all of the rode into the dinghy. Row or motor away, deploying the rode as you go. This avoids having to drag the line through the water and is most easily accomplished with two people in the dinghy. Return to the boat and set the second anchor in similar fashion.

ANCHORING TIPS

▶ Adjust two bow anchors so they pull evenly.

▶ Except for Med mooring, side tie the dinghy to the aft quarter when anchoring.

▶ To set two bow anchors under sail, lower the first anchor and reach across to the desired spot for the second anchor. Snub the predetermined scope of the first rode to set the anchor and tack. Lower the second anchor and reach back toward the first anchor, paying out the predetermined scope of the second rode. Snub the second rode to set the anchor. Lower the mainsail and drift backward, letting out both rodes to the desired scope.

Med Moor

Boats save docking space by anchoring with their sterns tied to a fixed pier. A plank (*pasarelle*) running from the shore to your stern provides access to and from the boat. This procedure, known as Mediterranean or Med mooring, requires close coordination between the helmsman and the crew and should be practiced beforehand. It is a difficult maneuver to perform in a crosswind.

Note the direction of the anchor rodes coming off moored boats. Prepare the anchor rode and stern mooring lines. Place fenders and tie the dinghy to the bow.

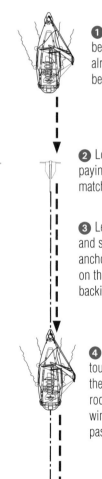

❶ Position the boat beyond the anchor rodes already deployed and begin backing up slowly.

❷ Lower the anchor, paying out the rode to match your speed.

❸ Let out about 4:1 scope and snub the rode to set anchor. Maintain pressure on the rode to keep boat backing in a straight line.

❹ Just short of touching the dock, cleat the anchor rode. As the rode comes taut, the windward stern line is passed to a dockhand.

❺ Set a second stern line on the opposite quarter and position the *pasarelle* (gangway or plank).

Unfouling Anchors

Sometimes anchor rodes foul or cross due to changing winds or currents or if another boat drags. With patience and cooperation, you can extract your anchor without mishap.

If two anchor rodes tangle, usually only one rode will hold both boats. Pass the least loaded line from the other boat and unwind it from the working rode until they're both free.

Dragging

Cleat the rode and put your hand or foot on it as the engine reverses. If you feel vibration or chattering, the anchor is dragging. Ease out more rode or raise the anchor and start over again. If it won't set, pick another location or use a different type of anchor.

If the bearings vary more than a few degrees as you swing, the anchor is dragging and needs to be reset.

After your anchor sets, take bearings on two or three fixed objects with the compass.

Do's & Don'ts

▶ Do note the direction and "lie" of other rodes before anchoring to avoid fouling.

▶ Don't continue raising your anchor if you encounter extraordinary resistance or your actions move a nearby boat. Instead, stop and assess the situation.

▶ Do use your dinghy to unwind fouled rodes.

▶ Don't cut or disconnect anyone's rode without their permission.

Raising an Anchor under Power

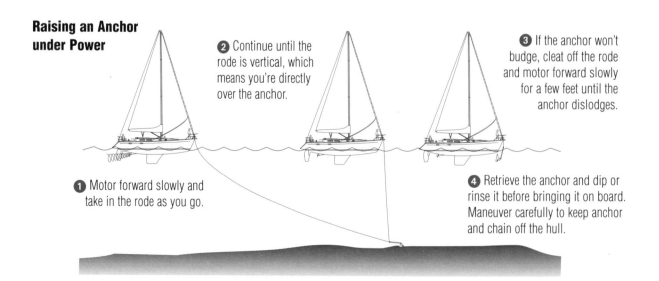

❷ Continue until the rode is vertical, which means you're directly over the anchor.

❸ If the anchor won't budge, cleat off the rode and motor forward slowly for a few feet until the anchor dislodges.

❶ Motor forward slowly and take in the rode as you go.

❹ Retrieve the anchor and dip or rinse it before bringing it on board. Maneuver carefully to keep anchor and chain off the hull.

Windlass

Many cruising boats use a windlass for raising the anchor. It can handle both rope and chain rodes. It is not designed to pull the boat forward or break the anchor free. Some windlasses operate manually with a lever and others are electrically powered. Running your engine while using an electric windlass will avoid draining your batteries. *Be sure your charter briefing is very thorough on windlass operation and always treat it with extreme caution.*

A well-placed windlass, bow roller and chain break make up an important part of the ground tackle system.

Ralph Naranjo photo

You operate a power windlass with a button in the deck or a hand control. Keep your clothing, hair and other body parts well clear of the gear mechanism. Never put your hands on the chain while the power is on.

Since an all-chain rode doesn't stretch, you should attach a piece of nylon line (snubber line) to the chain and tie it to the boat so it will absorb shock loads when anchored in strong wind and waves.

Using a Trip Line

A trip line, equal to the depth of the water at high tide plus five or ten feet, attaches to the *crown* of the anchor and leads to a buoy which floats directly over the anchor. If you anticipate trouble breaking the anchor free from a rocky or littered bottom, use the trip line to pull it from a different angle.

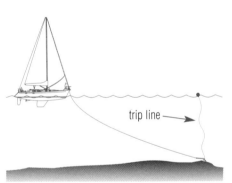

trip line →

Recovering a Rode under Another Boat

❶ When your rode crosses that of another boat, motor slowly in the direction of your rode and take up the slack.

❷ Stay clear of and pass around the other boat on the side of your rode. If your rode remains crossed, politely ask the other boat's skipper to motor forward on his rode until you can free your anchor.

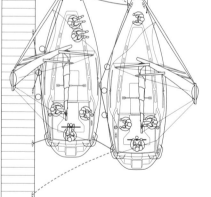

Mooring

Review hand signals before attempting to pick up a mooring pennant. You'll need a boat hook to lift a trailing pennant out of the water. Other pennants attached to pick-up poles can be reached easily from deck level. Pass a line through the eye splice, then secure the line to the boat. If the buoy ring lacks a pennant, use the boat hook to bring the buoy up close. Fasten one end of a line to the boat, pass the line through the ring and back to the boat.

Rafting

Successful rafting depends on cooperation and mutual consideration. Always wait to be invited, use your own fenders and make sure the spreaders don't line up.

Rafting at Anchor.

❶ First boat sets anchor before the second boat comes alongside.
❷ Deploy fenders and docklines to protect and control boats as they swing.
❸ Set additional anchors as needed. If a wind shift is anticipated, set an anchor at a 60 degree angle to the first anchor from the second boat.

Picking Up a Mooring

❸ Shift into reverse to stop the boat. Crew picks up the buoy pennant, keeping the buoy on the windward side of the boat. If you miss the pennant or the crew can't hold on, back away to keep the propeller away from the mooring and its pennant.

❷ Shift into neutral about two boat lengths from the buoy.

WIND

❶ Slowly motor upwind with crew ready at the bow and a second crew near midships as backup.

Rafting at Dock.

❶ Secure the first boat at dockside with spring lines, bow and stern lines, and several fenders.

❷ Bring the second boat alongside, with fenders in place, and secure to the first boat with spring, bow and stern lines. Watch your spreader alignment.

RAFTING CHECKLIST

▶ Place fenders high enough to protect topsides.
▶ Align boats fore and aft with spring lines so spreaders will not lock even if the boats roll.
▶ When walking across boats, go quietly forward of the mast.
▶ Inform other boats of your departure plans.
▶ Be considerate of other people's quiet hours after dark.

Underway with a Dinghy

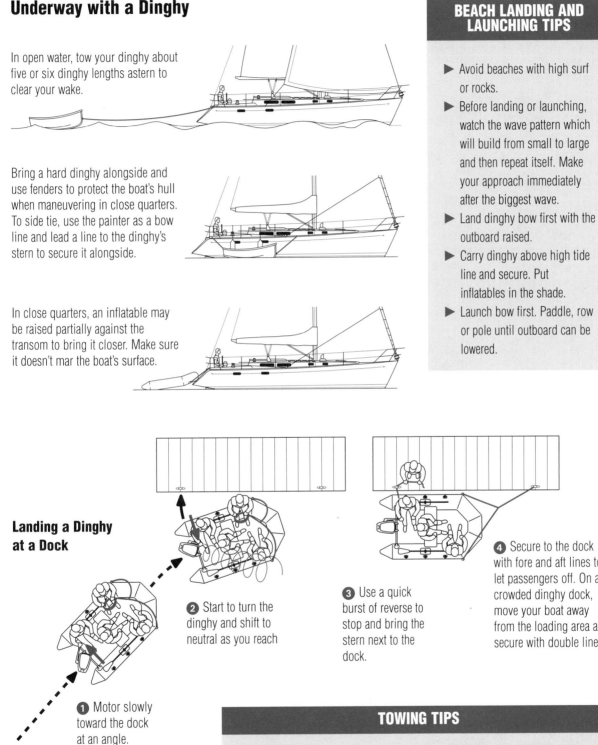

In open water, tow your dinghy about five or six dinghy lengths astern to clear your wake.

Bring a hard dinghy alongside and use fenders to protect the boat's hull when maneuvering in close quarters. To side tie, use the painter as a bow line and lead a line to the dinghy's stern to secure it alongside.

In close quarters, an inflatable may be raised partially against the transom to bring it closer. Make sure it doesn't mar the boat's surface.

BEACH LANDING AND LAUNCHING TIPS

▶ Avoid beaches with high surf or rocks.

▶ Before landing or launching, watch the wave pattern which will build from small to large and then repeat itself. Make your approach immediately after the biggest wave.

▶ Land dinghy bow first with the outboard raised.

▶ Carry dinghy above high tide line and secure. Put inflatables in the shade.

▶ Launch bow first. Paddle, row or pole until outboard can be lowered.

Landing a Dinghy at a Dock

1 Motor slowly toward the dock at an angle.

2 Start to turn the dinghy and shift to neutral as you reach

3 Use a quick burst of reverse to stop and bring the stern next to the dock.

4 Secure to the dock with fore and aft lines to let passengers off. On a crowded dinghy dock, move your boat away from the loading area and secure with double lines.

TOWING TIPS

▶ Remove gear, outboard and oars before towing unless otherwise directed by charter company.

▶ Proceed cautiously in high winds or towing across the wind, waves and wakes to avoid flooding or capsizing the dinghy.

▶ Retrieve towline before slowing or reversing the engine.

Living Aboard

Living together on a boat requires cooperation, patience and a sense of humor. In close quarters even minor habits can become annoying. Make sure everyone knows their responsibilities, so no one person does all the work.

Sharing a common area, each person still enjoys independent activity.

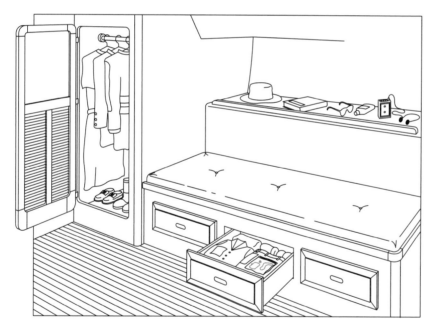

Keeping your personal gear in order is important in limited space. Use plastic bags to separate toiletries, jewelry, and other hard to find items. Pack clothes so the most used ones are on top.

ROTATION OF DUTIES

▶ Unless they're beyond someone's physical ability, all housekeeping jobs on the boat should be shared.

▶ Rotate assignments daily so everyone can play, relax, and sail equitably.

▶ Divide the tasks so they are of equal length.

▶ Remind everyone to do jobs at assigned times.

HOUSEKEEPING TIPS

▶ Leave no personal items in common areas.

▶ Dry wet items, including yourself, before going below.

▶ Wash off sand or salt water on deck.

▶ Run the shower water only to get wet and rinse off.

▶ Remove hair from shower drain after you shower.

▶ Scrape or wipe down plates before washing to conserve water.

▶ Clear away food and wash dishes promptly to avoid attracting insects.

Do's & Don'ts

▶ Do respect others' privacy.

▶ Do respect others' need for sleep if you are a night owl or early riser.

▶ Don't block a companionway by sunbathing or reading immediately in front of a hatch.

On Board Activities

While most charterers schedule two or three nights ashore for dinner, the bulk of your evening entertainment will be self-generated. Part of cruise planning should include creative ways to spend your leisure time. Consider, for example, one or two theme nights with costumes and impromptu performances.

Trash Management

Your charter office will tell you the proper procedure for disposing of trash. Treat all cruising areas with respect and don't pollute. To minimize trash accumulation remove and dispose of packaging before you leave the dock. Rinse cans, bottles and other containers with salt water before putting in the trash to reduce smell and insects. Crush aluminum cans. Remove both ends from tin cans and flatten the tubes. Fill rigid containers with other garbage before putting into trash. If you accumulate more than your trash container will hold, remove the plastic bag and put it downwind from your living area. Remember, plastic may never be thrown overboard in any ocean.

LEISURE ACTIVITY TIPS

▶ Plan some activities for evenings and quiet times. For children, bring favorite games, books or toys. To save space, set a limit on how much to bring.

▶ Musical instruments are excellent for sunset concerts, but be thoughtful of other people's quiet hours.

▶ Books you don't have time for at home make for good reading on a cruise.

▶ Playing cards offer many options for adults and children.

▶ Magnetic checkers, chess and backgammon travel anywhere.

▶ Knitting, needlework, and paints can unleash your creativity.

▶ Keeping a daily log or journal of your trip preserves your memories. School age children enjoy this activity too.

A large canvas bag with sturdy handles has many uses, including carrying ice, and stows easily.

Large blocks of ice can even be managed by children when there's a wheel barrow or wagon available.

HEAD ETIQUETTE

▶ Sharing the head calls for courtesy and tidiness.

▶ Use the head as quickly as possible in case others are waiting.

▶ Empty and leave the bowl clean.

▶ Make sure the toilet seat is down and clean.

▶ Wipe up water from counter top.

Multihulls

A multihull boat offers a different cruising and charter experience. Wide and stable, multihulls heel less, ride more smoothly and cut through waves with less effort than monohulls. Two hulls tend to make tacking slower. They also create more windage, which has to be compensated for when maneuvering under power.

Photo courtesy Catamaran Charters, Inc.

Less draft allows a multihull to cruise and anchor in shallower water than a monohull and can open up new cruising areas.

Multihull Features

▶ Separate hulls offer private sleeping accommodations.

▶ Salon and deck areas tend to be on the same level instead of being separated above and below decks.

▶ The spacious decks create more lounging area for the crew.

▶ Multihulls with an engine in each hull improve maneuverability.

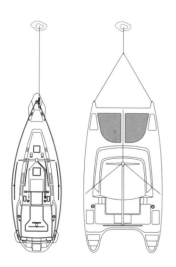

An anchor bridle distributes the anchor pull evenly between the two hulls and keeps the multihull square to the wind or current.

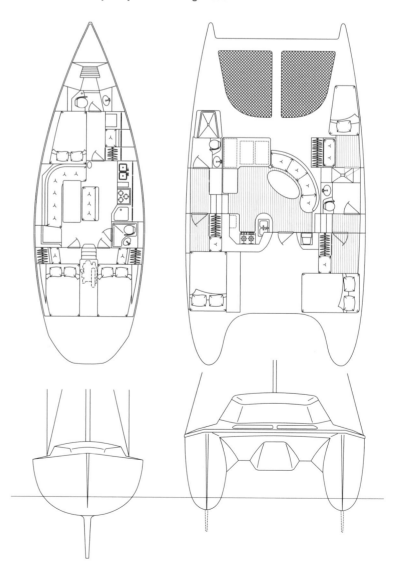

Protocols and Local Customs

Cruising in foreign countries offers the excitement of meeting people from a different culture. As a guest, your respect for their way of life will make you welcome. Ignoring or belittling local customs and practices can result in an unfriendly reception. Prepare yourself by learning something about your host country before your trip.

To check in, the boat's captain shows the local officials the boat's documents, passports for each person on board, a crew list, and clearance from the last port. You may also have to fill out an equipment declaration form noting electronics, firearms, liquor, tobacco and prescription drugs.

CHECKLIST

▶ Anchor or moor in designated area and hoist the yellow Q flag.

▶ Prepare at least three copies of boat papers, crew list, port clearance, and equipment declaration.

▶ Captain or owner goes ashore with official papers and all passports while the rest of the crew remain on board.

▶ After clearing, lower the Q flag and replace it with the national flag of your host country.

▶ Before departing, obtain an official clearance for your next port of call.

Upon arrival in a foreign country, fly the Q flag from your starboard spreader until you clear customs, immigration, and the port captain. After completing these formalities, lower the yellow Q flag and replace it with the recognized flag of your host country.

Do's & Don'ts

▶ Do learn a few words of the local language.

▶ Do conform with local customs and religions.

▶ Don't attempt to bribe local officials.

▶ Don't take any illegal substances on board. Foreign governments often treat drug offenders with harsh treatment, fines and jail terms.

▶ Do fly the national flag of your boat's registry from the stern when visiting a foreign country.

▶ Do fly the national flag of your host country, also called the courtesy flag, from the starboard spreader.

Navigation Rules

Refamiliarize yourself with the *Navigation Rules, International-Inland*. Your safe speed depends on visibility, traffic density and maneuverability. When two vessels under power are in a crossing situation, the one on the right is the stand-on vessel. When crossing traffic separation zones, it should be done with caution and at right angles. A vessel under sail usually has right-of-way over a vessel under power, except for vessels restricted in maneuverability or "engaged in fishing."

Under Sail

Sidelights are red on the port side and green on the starboard side, each with an arc of 112.5 degrees.

Sternlight is white with an arc of 135 degrees

Light Signals

Recognizing lights is important to your safety. When you can see both the red and green lights of another vessel, it's headed directly at you. If you see a white light above the green and/or red lights, the vessel is under power. A vessel at anchor will display a white 360 degrees anchor light from sunset to sunrise.

Under Power

Sidelights are red on the port side and green on the starboard side, each with an arc of 112.5 degrees.

Mast or steaming light faces forward with an arc of 225 degrees.

Sternlight is white with an arc of 135 degrees.

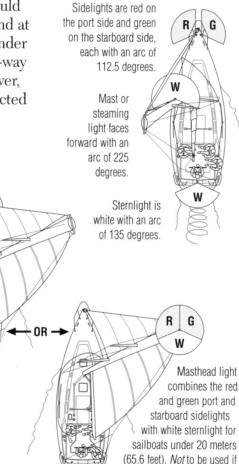

Masthead light combines the red and green port and starboard sidelights with white sternlight for sailboats under 20 meters (65.6 feet). *Not* to be used if sidelights and sternlight are lit, or while motoring.

Sound Signals

For vessels in sight of each other:
● One short blast indicates *altering* course to starboard (International), or *intending* to alter course to starboard (Inland) when meeting or crossing.
●● Two short blasts indicate *altering* course to port (International), or *intending* to alter course to port (Inland) when meeting or crossing.
●●● Three short blasts indicate engine is in reverse (although vessel may still be moving forward).
●●●●● Five short blasts = danger.

For vessels in restricted visibility:
— One prolonged blast every two minutes indicates a vessel under power.
— ●● One prolonged blast followed by two short blasts every two minutes indicates a vessel under sail. Be aware that other vessels will also sound this signal, e.g., vessels engaged in towing, fishing, pushing, and vessels restricted in their ability to maneuver.

Other sound signals:
— One prolonged blast shall be sounded by a vessel nearing a bend of a channel or fairway where other vessels may be obscured.

▶ For other sound signals (e.g., overtaking signals) consult the *Navigation Rules, International-Inland*.

▶ A short blast is about one second's duration and a prolonged blast is from four to six seconds' duration.

▶ Nowadays, most ships routinely rely on bridge to bridge radio communication to make passing arrangements. This reduces the confusion generated by traditional sound signals in heavy traffic where it may be unclear who is being hailed. Monitoring bridge to bridge radio communication is an excellent way to gain awareness of potential ship traffic. Check with your charter company or local knowledge for radio channels used in your area.

Day Shapes

During daytime, the Navigation Rules require sailboats anchored outside a designated anchorage to display a black ball shape. A sailboat under power and with sails up should display an inverted cone, unless it's less than 12 meters (39.4 feet) in Inland waters. The white and blue "alpha" code flag is the internationally recognized signal for a diver in the water, although a red flag with a white diagonal stripe is often used in U.S. waters.

The Intracoastal Waterway

Sailors on the East Coast of the United States and the Gulf of Mexico should be aware of the Intracoastal Waterway (ICW), also called "The Ditch." This protected waterway uses its own, unique markings. When following the ICW from New Jersey to Texas, a yellow ▲ should be left to starboard and a yellow ■ to port, *regardless of the color of the navigation aid on which they appear.* The prudent navigator will follow charts closely and carry an up-to-date ICW cruising guide.

The Intracoastal Waterway is a network of protected inland water routes winding from New Jersey to Texas

Since there is no obvious approach from seaward for the Intracoastal waterway, the Conventional Direction of clockwise rotation around the U.S. land mass is used. As a result, the marks toward the mainland side of the waterway are designated as marking the right side of the Waterway, and the ones toward the sea are the left side (see below).

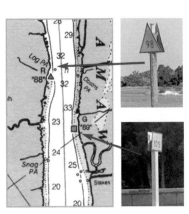

The yellow triangle on this red daymark indicates the starboard (mainland) side of the ICW channel.

The yellow square on this green daymark marks the port (seaward) side of the ICW channel.

There are places along the ICW where the Waterway and a channel leading in from the sea coincide. If the directions of the two systems are the same, the yellow triangles will be on the red starboard marks and the yellow squares on green port marks. But if the conventional direction of the Waterway

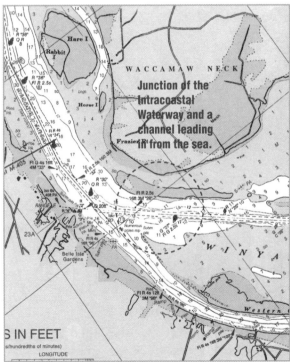

Junction of the Intracoastal Waterway and a channel leading in from the sea.

system runs opposite to the "returning from seaward" direction of the channel , the U.S. Marking system for the channel prevails and the yellow triangles will be on channel's green marks and the yellow squares on the red marks. Extreme care should be exercised when passing the junction of the Intracoastal Waterway and a channel leading in from the sea. The mixture of marks can be very confusing, but if you follow the yellow ICW symbols, you should not get lost.

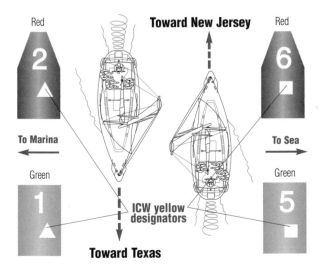

The Chart

Charts form the core of all navigation. They are a two-dimensional depiction of a three-dimensional reality. With great accuracy they show an area of sea and its associated land with any undersea and topographical features important for navigation.

The coastline is obvious on a chart, with sea and land clarified by self-explanatory color-coding. The small numbers scattered throughout the water are soundings, or depths, at those particular points on the chart. Everything else is shown in symbolic form. The meanings of most symbols should be clear. If in doubt, consult NOAA (National Oceanic and Atmospheric Administration) chart #1.

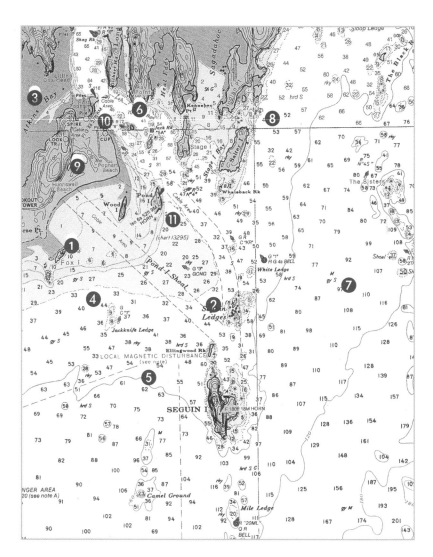

Chart Alternatives

In many areas, private companies issue charts which can be a useful alternative to those published by NOAA. *Chart Books* come in handy packages sized for a small chart table. *Imray-Iolaire* charts of the Caribbean are specially designed for the yachting user and often include harbor plans as insets.

Additional Information

By their nature, charts can give only a two-dimensional picture. This can be expanded by referring to *Coast Pilots,* the official companions to the U.S. Chart. *Coast Pilots* contain information including descriptions of the coastline and port details. For sailing directions relevant to small craft, a yachtsman's *Cruising Guide* is useful. These vary in quality, but a good one is an essential companion in unfamiliar waters. In case your charts are out of date, a current *Light List* is valuable. This will also fill you in on recognition features of light structures. For additional information, refer to US SAILING's *Coastal Navigation.* Local cruising guides can also be a useful addition to your charts in unfamiliar waters.

❶ The vertical lettering of Fox I. indicates it's dry at high water.

The slant lettering of Sequin Ledges ❷ indicates it's submerged.

Green color (on original chart) indicates Atkins Bay drys out at low tide and its extent is shown by the dotted line ❸.

Underwater contour lines ❹ are called *depth curves* or *fathom curves.* Typically a harbor chart will have a 6-foot line and coastal charts 12, 18 or 30-foot lines.

❺ This indicates a magnetic disturbance which will affect your compass reading.

Tide rips ❻ indicate rough water.

❼ Symbols indicate the type of bottom

is mud (M) and grey (gy) sand (S).

This sounding in brackets ❽ indicate it's out of position.

Contour lines of this hill ❾ indicate its height above datum. Lines closely spaced indicate a steep rise.

❿ Landmarks, such as lookout towers, spires and cupolas, are useful navigational references.

Charts indicate the characteristics and location of navigation aids. The symbols ⓫ indicate this lighthouse has an isophase light (equal light and dark intervals) flashing every 6 seconds, 52 feet high with a 9 mile visibility, as well as a foghorn.

Distance, Speed & Time

Position on a chart is defined by lines running vertically, known as *longitude*, and their horizontal counterparts called *latitude*.

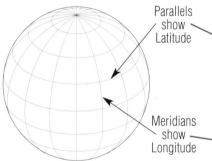

Parallels show Latitude

Meridians show Longitude

Latitude is measured in degrees 0 to 90 north or south from the equator, while **longitude** is designated from 0 to 180 degrees east or west from Greenwich, England.

A degree is divided into 60 subdivisions known as *minutes* (nothing to do with time!) with a minute of latitude equal to one Nautical Mile – approximately 2000 yards.

Distance traveled through the water is measured by a *log*. This instrument may be electronic with a digital read-out of speed as well as distance run, promising accuracy to two decimal places. It can alternatively be a towed spinner activating a simple analogue dial showing distance only. Either can be accurate, depending on siting, maintenance and sea state. Do not expect perfection.

Speed ties time to distance, just as it does on land or in the air. Speed at sea is measured in *knots*, which are nautical miles per hour.

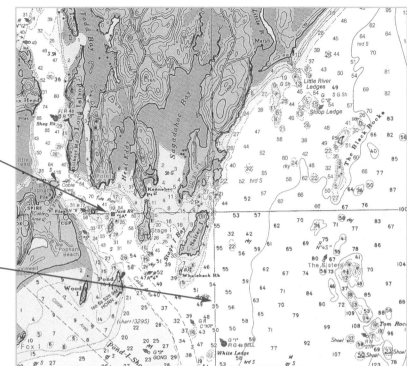

A Mercator chart (above) shows lines of longitude *(meridians)* running parallel, but in reality they are closing together, finally meeting at the poles (see above). The *parallels* of latitude are equidistant.

To measure distance on a chart, place your dividers across it, then transfer the span to the latitude scale on the *side* of the chart. Note the minutes of latitude, and that is your distance in miles and tenths of a mile. Distance Ⓐ is 3.4 miles.

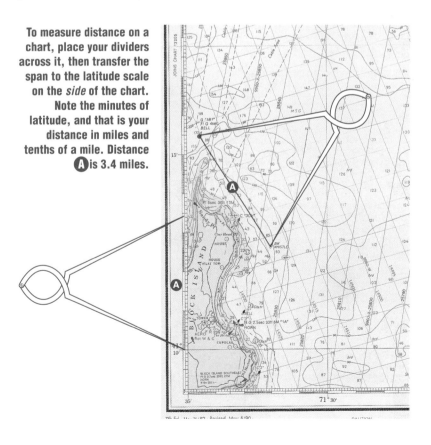

Direction

It is vital that the navigator can define accurately the direction from one point on the chart to another. While the old north, south, east and west nomenclature still holds good for purposes such as wind direction or remarks about a boat's general heading, any accurate statement is given in degrees. This is achieved by means of a "360° in a circle" notation corresponding to the way in which courses and bearings are now established.

The purest form of course and bearing measurement lines up zero degrees with any meridian of longitude. The reading thus obtained is unaffected by those considerations which affect the magnetic compass and is given in degrees *True (T)*.

Some navigators prefer to use parallel rulers rather than a plotter, reading off all courses and bearings in Magnetic on the chart, and never using True at all. This is fine, so long as you remember that any courses or bearings printed on the chart or given in pilot books are generally in degrees True. Tidal current information is always given in degrees True.

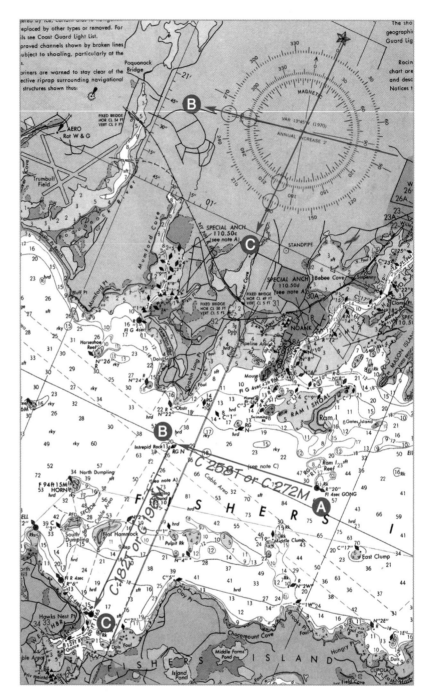

With an up-to-date chart and either a plotter or parallel rulers you can determine the courses to steer from point Ⓐ to point Ⓑ and from Ⓑ to Ⓒ By transferring the proposed course lines from A to B and B to C to the compass rose, you can determine the directions in either degrees True (outer ring) or degrees Magnetic (inner ring) by reading the circled headings at the letters Ⓑ and Ⓒ. The headings for the course to steer are written alongside their course lines with a capital "C" in front to indicate it's a course, e.g., C 258 T (degrees True) and C 272 M (degrees Magnetic) for the A to B line (normally either C 258 T or C 272 M would be written, not both).

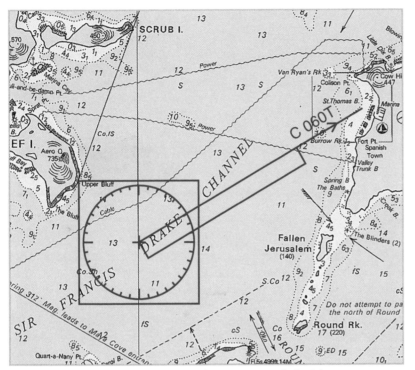

Reproduced from Imray-Iolaire chart A 232 by permission of Imray Laurie Norie and Wilson Ltd

Plotting a Course to Steer

◀ A line joining the yacht's position and the point she wants to go to is called a *course to steer*. In this case, with the plotter body correctly oriented to a meridian and the plotter arm lined up with the course line, the course is 060 degrees True (T).

Courses and bearings are expressed in a 3-figure notation and can be plotted in degrees True or Magnetic (see p. 70) using either parallel rulers or a plotter.

Plotting a Bearing

Some navigators prefer to use parallel rulers in conjunction with the compass rose on the chart (see below). In this case they are determining a bearing (the line joining a known point with the yacht's position), not a course line. The bearing is either 314 degrees True (T) - outer ring number or 330 degrees Magnetic (M) - inner ring number. ▼

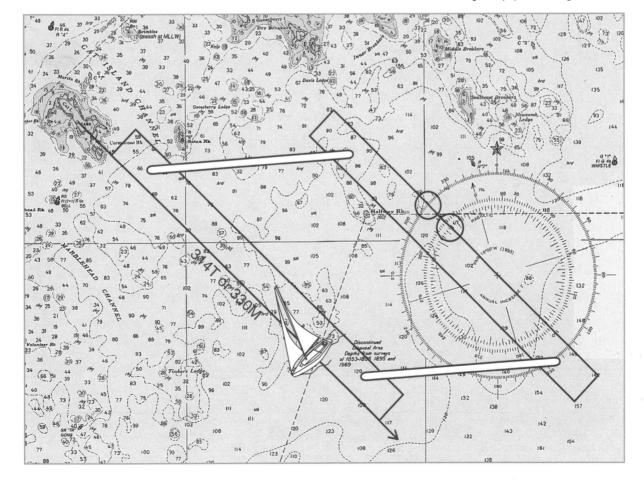

The Steering Compass

A yacht compass allows you to use the Earth's magnetic field as a reference for steering your boat. There are a few factors to be aware of, however, before you start using your compass for precise positioning of your boat on a chart.

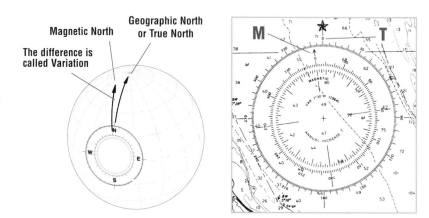

Deviation

Some yacht steering compasses are subject to deviation resulting from permanent magnetically active items on board. This is not usually encountered in bareboat fleets but if you charter a boat that does have this feature you should discover a deviation card in the navigation station. Deviation alters on different headings, so the card sets out how many degrees east or west of any magnetic heading the yacht's compass reads. This may be in the form of a graph (see inset diagram) or it could be a table. To apply deviation, use a diagram like the one used for variation (inset), but start with the *magnetic* heading as the datum point. A magnetic course adjusted for deviation is known as a compass course and is designated in degrees with the letter "C." Example: **230 C**.

NOTE: *Temporary deviation can be caused by placing magnetically active items by the compass, such as batteries, portable stereos, tools and air-horns.*

Variation

A compass lines itself up with the Earth's magnetic field, and it points to the *magnetic* North Pole, which is actually different from the *true* geographic North pole (above left). Compass bearings are therefore Magnetic (**M**), and the amount and direction by which the compass varies from True North (**T**) is noted by an inner circle (True) and outer circle (Magnetic) on the chart's compass rose (above right). You can navigate using the magnetic rose alone, taking off courses and bearings with parallel rulers. Some plotters can read in Magnetic as well as True, and these are very useful. Sometimes, however, you may come across charts that do not show a magnetic rose, or find yourself with a plotter which reads in True only. If so, you must convert your True course to Magnetic before giving them up to the helmsman. Conversely, any magnetic bearings passed down to the navigator must be converted to True for plotting.

Correcting for Variation

If you need to do this and are in doubt about whether to add or subtract variation, draw a scratch diagram as shown. Because in this case the line **T** joining the yacht's heading to the True North sweeps through less arc than **M**, which indicates the magnetic arc, you can see that the Magnetic version of the course or bearing will be greater than the True. Thus, west variation must be added to convert the True reading to Magnetic, or subtracted to go from Magnetic to True. East variation would be the other way around.

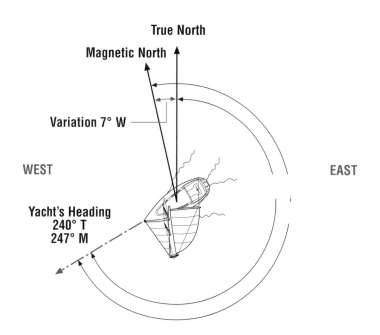

Depth

After distance and direction, depth is the third navigational dimension.

If you inspect any chart, you will notice the water is dotted with small numbers called *soundings*. In some places soundings represent "lower low water," a lower than average tide. In others it may represent mean (average) low water. If tide is going to be a significant factor, check near the chart title to see which "datum" is used.

Traditionally, soundings are measured in fathoms (1 fathom = 6 feet) and feet. Shallower water is recorded as fathoms with a subscript indicating additional foot increments. For example, 4 fathoms and 3 feet = 27 feet, which would be shown as 4_3. Charts of very shallow water may be sounded in feet only (see example at right).

There is a steady evolution in charts towards showing the internationally accepted "meters" for depth and height. A metric chart is sounded in meters and tenths of a meter. One meter = 3 feet 3 inches (approx.).

In tidal waters, some areas are dry at low water. Depths here are charted with a line underneath them, as *drying heights* above the chart datum.

Every chart states the nature of its soundings (fathoms, feet, meters or combinations) near the title. Read it, and take heed!

Depths are often measured by an instrument called a *fathometer,* which emits signals from a through-hull transducer mounted below the waterline. The fathometer may read depth below its through-hull transducer, below keel, or overall depth. Check to be sure.

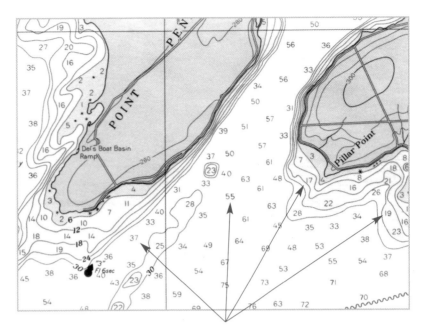

On this chart, soundings represent depth at mean low water.

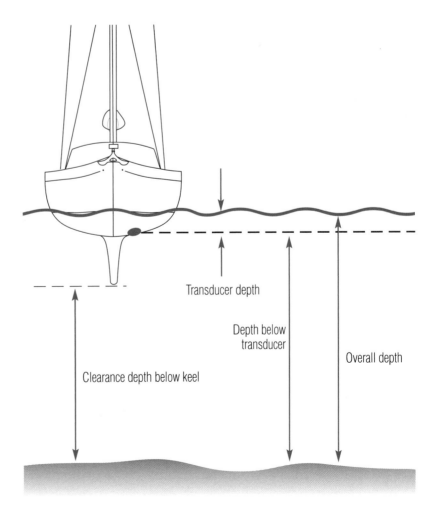

Transducer depth

Depth below transducer

Overall depth

Clearance depth below keel

Tidal Heights

Because tides are pulled by the gravity of the moon and sun, they rise higher (and fall lower) when both bodies are in line with the earth. This happens twice a month at full moon and new moon. At these times, *spring tides* occur (no connection with the seasons at all). At half moon, tides are literally half the size and are called *neaps*.

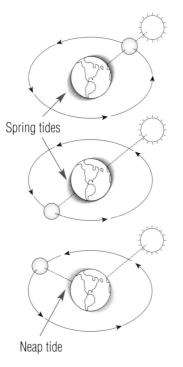

Spring tides

Neap tide

You can find the times and heights of high and low water for any day at a standard station (major port) by looking in the tide tables. These are reproduced in tide tables or nautical almanacs and are generally available locally from charter operators or chandlers. The heights are to be *added* to charted depths to discover the actual depth at a given place at high or low water. Remember to check on the chart near the title to find what chart datum is used (meters, feet, fathoms, etc). Occasionally, a spring low water may appear as a negative figure. This means that the depth of water will be *less than the charted depth* by that amount.

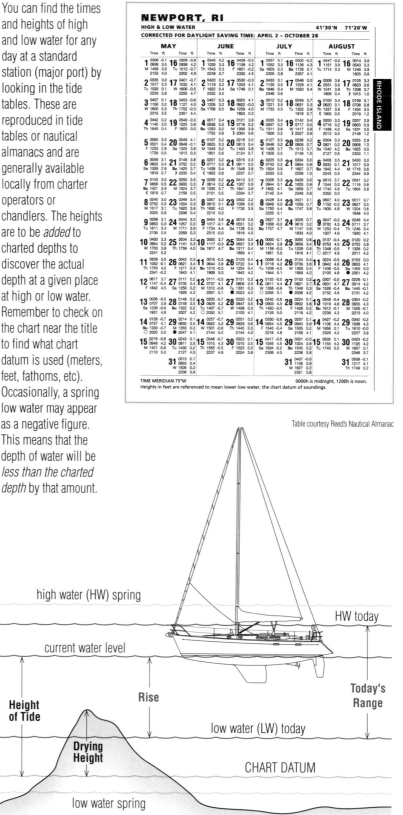

Table courtesy Reed's Nautical Almanac

high water (HW) spring

HW today

current water level

Rise

Today's Range

Height of Tide

low water (LW) today

Drying Height

CHART DATUM

low water spring

The Rule of Twelfths

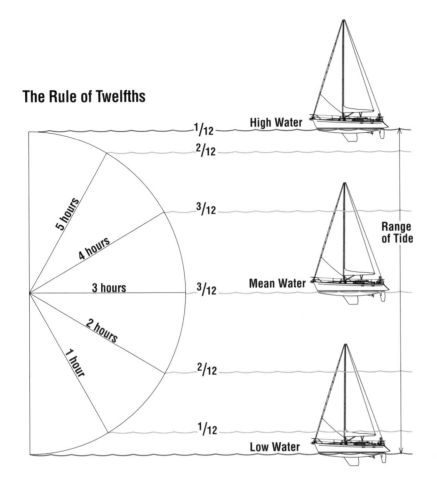

To work out the height of tide at a time between high and low water, you must first calculate the *range* of that particular tide. This is simply the difference between high and low water.

e.g.

	HW	8 feet
-	LW	2 feet
	Range	6 feet

Now divide the range by 12 and apply the *Rule of Twelfths*. Using the Rule of Twelfths, 1/12 of the tide range rises in the first hour, 2 in the second, 3 in the third, 3 in the fourth, 2 in the fifth and 1 in the sixth hour of the tide. The water falls at a corresponding rate on the ebb.

This gives the *rise* of tide at the hour you want. **Add this figure to the low water height** on your chart or table which is always with you for the duration of the tide, and you have the height of tide for the time of your interest.

Example:
The rise of the tide after 4 hrs. would be:
Range = 6 feet
$\frac{1}{12} \times 6 = \frac{1}{2}$ foot
4 hours = $\frac{1}{12} + \frac{2}{12} + \frac{3}{12} + \frac{3}{12} = \frac{9}{12}$

Rise after 4 hrs. = $\frac{9}{12} \times 6$ feet = 4.5 feet
(or $9 \times \frac{1}{2}$ foot = 4.5 feet)
Add 4.5 feet to LW height to find height of tide

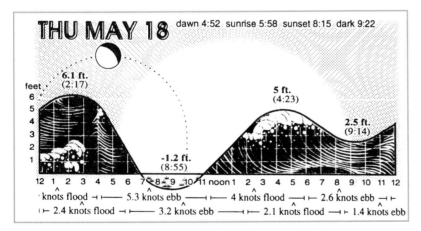

Some areas (e.g. San Francisco Bay) issue useful tidal height graphs which may be used as an alternative to the Rule of Twelfths. These are simple and accurate. Always remember, however, that tidal calculations are based on *predictions* and that water levels may prove to be different on the day. courtesy Tidelog®, © 1995 Pacific Publishers

Secondary Stations
Stations of secondary commercial importance are not fully tabulated, but are referred to a convenient standard port. Such stations are found in the almanac next to the standard port, together with information known as *tidal differences*. Height information for the standard port is multiplied by the *ratio* to find the equivalent data for the secondary station. Time differences are self-explanatory.

Tidal Currents

Tidal currents are the *horizontal* movement of water caused by the gravitational pull of the moon and sun on the earth. An incoming tidal current is sail to be "flooding" and an outgoing tidal current is said to be "ebbing." During Spring tides, tidal current velocities are greatest.

Tidal currents (sometimes called *streams*) are tabulated in tidal current tables, nautical almanacs, or local publications. The information may also be presented in *current tables* or *tidal current charts* with arrows indicating strength and direction of the water movement.

Current Tables (see table at right) are easy to read, giving the times of slack water (when tides change from ebbing to flooding or vice versa), maximum current, and the general direction and specific strength in knots for each day.

Approximately 3 hours elapse between slack water and maximum rate of flood or ebb. You can approximate the strength of an incoming or outgoing current by using the 1/3, 2/3, 3/3, 2/3, 1/3 rule (see "The Rule of Twelfths" on page 73). At 1 hour after slack, the current runs at 1/3 of maximum, 2 hours after, it is up to 2/3. At three hours, the current is running at maximum, or 3/3. The current then slackens off at the same rate, with strength 4 hours after slack at 2/3, etc. (see example at right)

THE RACE, LONG ISLAND SOUND

CURRENT TABLE 1996 **FLOOD 302° EBB 112°**

CORRECTED FOR DAYLIGHT SAVING TIME: APRIL 7 – OCTOBER 26

JULY

Day	Slack time	Max time	Fld/Ebb knots
1 M	0613, 1220, 1823	0255, 0903, 1518, 2120	4.2, 3.6, 3.7, 3.8
2 Tu	0035, 0702, 1311, 1916	0345, 0953, 1610, 2211	4.3, 3.7, 3.8, 3.8
3 W	0126, 0752, 1403, 2011	0436, 1044, 1702, 2304	4.3, 3.7, 3.8, 3.6
4 Th	0219, 0843, 1456, 2107	0527, 1136, 1756, 2358	4.1, 3.7, 3.7, 3.4
5 F	0314, 0936, 1552, 2207	0620, 1229, 1851	3.9, 3.5, 3.6
6 Sa	0412, 1031, 1649, 2309	0055, 0715, 1324, 1949	3.1, 3.5, 3.2, 3.4
7 Su	0512, 1128, 1749	0154, 0813, 1422, 2049	2.8, 3.0, 3.0, 3.2
8 M	0013, 0616, 1228, 1849	0257, 0912, 1523, 2149	2.5, 2.9, 2.8, 3.1
9 Tu	0117, 0719, 1328, 1948	0403, 1013, 1626, 2250	2.4, 2.7, 2.7, 3.0
10 W	0218, 0821, 1426, 2044	0510, 1112, 1727, 2347	2.3, 2.6, 2.6, 3.0
11 Th	0315, 0918, 1521, 2136	0611, 1208, 1822	2.3, 2.6, 2.6
12 F	0406, 1010, 1611, 2223	0039, 0704, 1259, 1910	3.1, 2.4, 2.6, 2.6
13 Sa	0453, 1056, 1656, 2307	0126, 0748, 1345, 1952	3.1, 2.5, 2.6, 2.6
14 Su	0535, 1139, 1738, 2347	0209, 0826, 1428, 2030	3.2, 2.5, 2.7, 2.6
15 M ●	0614, 1219, 1818	0249, 0900, 1508, 2107	3.2, 2.6, 2.7, 2.6
16 Tu	0025, 0650, 1256, 1856	0328, 0935, 1547, 2144	3.2, 2.6, 2.8, 2.6
17 W	0101, 0726, 1332, 1934	0406, 1010, 1626, 2222	3.2, 2.6, 2.8, 2.6
18 Th	0137, 0800, 1408, 2012	0445, 1047, 1706, 2301	3.1, 2.7, 2.8, 2.6
19 F	0213, 0836, 1445, 2053	0524, 1126, 1747, 2343	3.0, 2.6, 2.7, 2.5
20 Sa	0251, 0913, 1523, 2137	0605, 1207, 1831	2.8, 2.6, 2.7
21 Su	0333, 0953, 1605, 2225	0027, 0649, 1251, 1917	2.3, 2.7, 2.5, 2.6
22 M	0420, 1038, 1652, 2318	0115, 0736, 1339, 2008	2.2, 2.5, 2.5, 2.6
23 Tu ☾	0513, 1128, 1745	0207, 0828, 1431, 2102	2.2, 2.4, 2.5, 2.7
24 W	0613, 1224, 1843	0303, 0924, 1526, 2200	2.1, 2.4, 2.5, 2.8
25 Th	0717, 1323, 1944	0403, 1023, 1625, 2258	2.2, 2.5, 2.6, 3.0
26 F	0219, 0821, 1424, 2043	0503, 1122, 1724, 2356	2.4, 2.7, 2.9, 3.4
27 Sa	0317, 0921, 1523	0602, 1220, 1821	2.7, 3.0, 3.1
28 Su	0412, 1017, 1620, 2235	0051, 0659, 1315, 1917	3.7, 3.1, 3.3, 3.4
29 M	0503, 1110, 1715, 2328	0144, 0752, 1408, 2011	4.0, 3.4, 3.7, 3.7
30 Tu ○	0553, 1203, 1808	0236, 0844, 1500, 2103	4.2, 3.7, 3.9, 3.8
31 W	0020, 0642, 1252, 1901	0326, 0934, 1552, 2155	4.4, 3.8, 4.1, 3.9

AUGUST

Day	Slack time	Max time	Fld/Ebb knots
1 Th	0111, 0731, 1343, 1954	0416, 1024, 1643, 2246	4.3, 3.9, 4.1, 3.7
2 F	0202, 0820, 1434, 2048	0506, 1114, 1734, 2338	4.2, 3.8, 3.9, 3.5
3 Sa	0255, 0911, 1526, 2144	0557, 1204, 1827	3.9, 3.5, 3.7
4 Su	0349, 1004, 1621, 2243	0031, 1257	3.2, 3.5, 3.2, 3.4
5 M	0447, 1059, 1718, 2344	0127, 0745, 1352, 2019	2.8, 3.1, 2.9, 3.1
6 Tu ☾	0548, 1158, 1818	0227, 0843, 1451, 2119	2.4, 2.7, 2.6, 2.9
7 W	0047, 0651, 1259, 1918	0331, 0943, 1553, 2219	2.2, 2.5, 2.4, 2.8
8 Th	0150, 0753, 1359, 2016	0440, 1044, 1657, 2318	2.1, 2.4, 2.3, 2.7
9 F	0248, 0852, 1456, 2110	0545, 1142, 1756	2.1, 2.4, 2.3
10 Sa	0340, 0944, 1547, 2159	0013, 0639, 1234, 1847	2.8, 2.2, 2.4, 2.4
11 Su	0427, 1031, 1634, 2243	0101, 0723, 1321, 1929	2.9, 2.3, 2.6, 2.5
12 M	0508, 1113, 1716, 2323	0144, 0800, 1403, 2007	3.0, 2.5, 2.7, 2.6
13 Tu	0546, 1151, 1755	0224, 0834, 1443, 2043	3.1, 2.6, 2.8, 2.7
14 W ●	0001, 0622, 1227, 1832	0302, 0907, 1521, 2119	3.2, 2.7, 2.9, 2.7
15 Th	0037, 0656, 1302, 1909	0339, 0942, 1559, 2156	3.2, 2.8, 3.0, 2.7
16 F	0112, 0729, 1335, 1945	0417, 1017, 1637, 2234	3.2, 2.8, 3.0, 2.7
17 Sa	0147, 0802, 1410, 2023	0455, 1055, 1717, 2314	3.1, 2.8, 3.0, 2.7
18 Su	0223, 0838, 1446, 2105	0534, 1135, 1758, 2357	2.9, 2.8, 2.9, 2.6
19 M	0303, 0917, 1527, 2151	0617, 1218, 1844	2.8, 2.7, 2.9
20 Tu	0348, 1002, 1614, 2244	0044, 0704, 1305, 1934	2.4, 2.6, 2.6, 2.8
21 W ☾	0441, 1054, 1709, 2344	0136, 0756, 1358, 2030	2.3, 2.5, 2.5, 2.8
22 Th	0543, 1153, 1812	0233, 0854, 1457, 2130	2.2, 2.4, 2.5, 2.8
23 F	0049, 0651, 1258, 1918	0335, 0957, 1559, 2232	2.3, 2.5, 2.6, 3.0
24 Sa	0153, 0758, 1405, 2023	0438, 1059, 1702, 2333	2.5, 2.7, 2.8, 3.3
25 Su	0254, 0901, 1508, 2123	0541, 1200, 1803	2.8, 3.1, 3.1
26 M	0351, 0958, 1606, 2220	0031, 0639, 1257, 1901	3.6, 3.1, 3.5, 3.4
27 Tu	0443, 1051, 1701, 2313	0125, 0734, 1351, 1956	4.0, 3.5, 3.8, 3.7
28 W ○	0533, 1142, 1754	0217, 0825, 1442, 2047	4.2, 3.8, 4.1, 3.8
29 Th	0004, 0621, 1231, 1845	0307, 0914, 1532, 2137	4.3, 3.9, 4.2, 3.9
30 F	0054, 0708, 1319, 1935	0355, 1002, 1621, 2226	4.2, 3.9, 4.2, 3.7
31 Sa	0143, 0756, 1408, 2026	0443, 1049, 1710, 2315	4.0, 3.7, 4.0, 3.5

TIME MERIDIAN 75°W   0000h is midnight, 1200h is noon.

1996 EAST COAST   3.69

Table courtesy Reed's Nautical Almanac

Example:

To determine the velocity and direction of current at The Race, Long Island Sound at 1330 hours, August 29, find the following information on the table (see arrow):

Time of slack water = 1231 hours

Maximum current at 1532 hours = 4.2 knots and ebbing (going out)

The interval between slack water and the desired time is

1330 - 1231 = 59 minutes or nearly 1 hour

The current velocity and direction at 1330 hours is

1/3 x 4.2 = 1.4 knots and ebbing

Tides & Currents

Reading Current

Running aground is a serious conse-
quence of being offset by a current. Each
time you pass by a fixed object in the
water, observe the direction (set) and
velocity (drift) of the current.

**The three-knot current shown pushing
on this buoy, causes it to lean and
leaves a wake as it flows from left to
right.** Photo courtesy Anne Martin

Tidal Current Charts come in sets of 11 or 12, related to hours before or after high
water at the local standard station or port. These chart samples show current coming in
(flooding) and going out *(ebbing)* of Long Island Sound. Rates are given for spring (big)
tides. For lesser tidal ranges, divide the rate by the spring range, then multiply it by the
range for the day. In practice, you can often make a satisfactory guess. Enter the tide
tables for the standard station to read off time and range of high water, and away you go.

chart courtesy Reed's Nautical Almanac

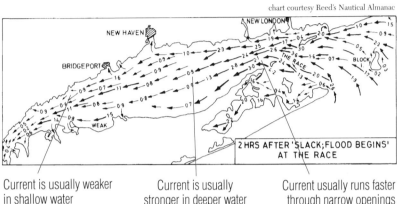

Current is usually weaker
in shallow water

Current is usually
stronger in deeper water

Current usually runs faster
through narrow openings

Example:

If current is given on a tidal current chart as 2 knots, and the spring range is 4 feet and
today's range is 3 feet (see page 72 for daily range calculation), today's current at this
hour would be: $\frac{2 \text{ knots} \times 3 \text{ feet}}{4 \text{ feet}} = 1.5 \text{ knots}$

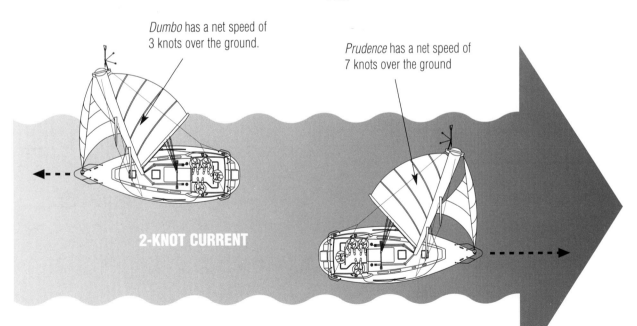

Dumbo has a net speed of
3 knots over the ground.

Prudence has a net speed of
7 knots over the ground

2-KNOT CURRENT

Using Current

Depending on their direction, currents can either assist or hinder your progress. Always try to sail with
the current if you can. This illustration shows two boats reaching at 5 knots with and against a 2-knot
current. *Prudence* uses the current to achieve a net speed of 7 knots (5+2) over the ground that more
than doubles *Dumbo's* net speed of 3 knots (5-2).

Plotting a Course to Compensate for Current

Draw a line 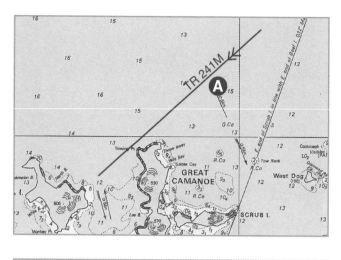ⓐ from your position to your destination. This is called the *track*. It is marked with two arrows and is sometimes formally labeled "TR" with a compass heading written along it. If you opt for this, always write "M" for Magnetic, "T" for True, or "C" for Compass after your numbers. The professional convention is always to work in True, so if no letter is noted, the degrees are assumed to be degrees True.

Deduce from your tidal current chart the probable *set* (direction) and *drift* (speed) of the stream for the next hour. Draw the *tidal vector line* ⓑ from your departure point in the direction of the *set*. Its length is determined by the *drift*, so that for a stream of one knot the line is one mile long. Mark the line with three arrows or formally label it "S D".

Estimate probable boat speed over the next hour and set up that number of miles on your dividers. Place one leg of the dividers on the end of your tidal vector and make a mark on the track line (TR) with the other. Join these two points with a third line ⓒ and give it a single arrow. This is your *course to steer*. DO NOT join the end of the tidal vector with your destination. The course line will fail to coincide with boat speed and the diagram will not work. If you want to label the course line formally, write "C" along it (for course), and the actual course steered in numbers of degrees (T, C or M). Motorboat skippers who know how fast they will be going write their boat speed along the other side of the line, but for a sailor, this is not required because you never know what your ultimate speed will be.

The easiest way to make clear what the various plotted lines mean is to stick simply to the arrows. If you ever need to know what the track is in degrees, it is an easy job to get it with your plotter. The only exception to this is course to steer. If you are not using a ship's log book (see page 80), it will pay you to note the heading on the course line so that the helmsman can check it if need be.

Note that the yacht stays on track all the way. If the passage is more or less than an hour, don't worry. So long as the track passes through your destination, you will arrive.

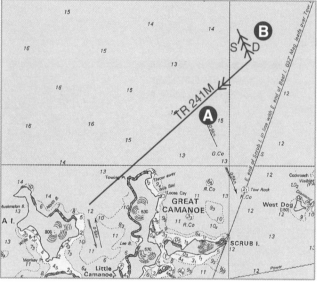

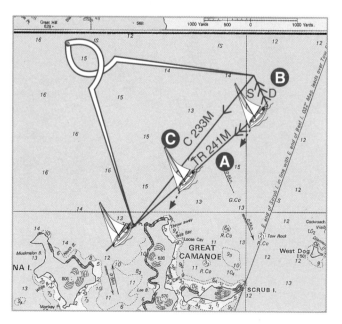

Charts on p. 76-77 reproduced from Imray-Iolaire chart A 232 by permission of Imray Laurie Norie and Wilson Ltd.

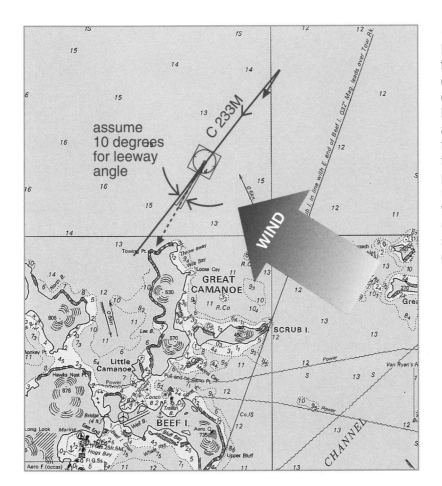

assume
10 degrees
for leeway
angle

◀ Compensating for Wind

If you are not sailing downwind, you will typically be blown to leeward of your course by five to ten degrees. This is called *leeway*. Leeway increases if the boat is moving slowly, has a small keel and rudder, or is heeled with the rail in the water. Leeway will also increase as the wind increases. To counteract it, place your plotter on the course line and rotate it, say ten degrees, toward the wind. Plot a short line with an arrowhead on the end of it. That is the course you should steer and will be the course entered in your ship's log book.

When your passage is of two hours or more, draw each hour's tide at the beginning as shown, then make your course line good for, in this case, 3 hours ▼

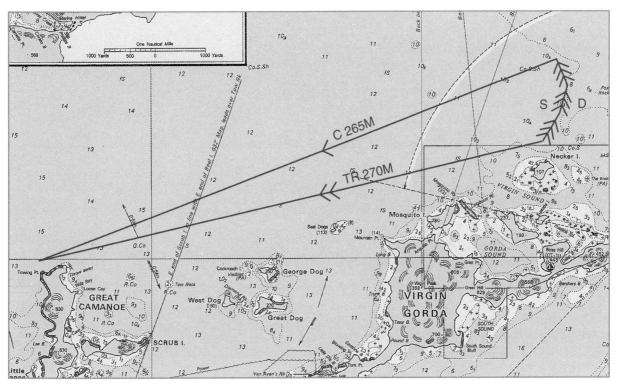

Finding Out Where You Are

The question of where you are can be solved in a number of ways. The most accurate of these is the electronic fix (see page 81), while at the other end of the scale is a good look around and an educated guess made after studying the chart. In between these two are a number of other methods.

Eyeball Positions

Take a look at the chart and try to relate it to what you see on the water. Your notes (or your log) will tell you how far you've come from your last position, and the compass shows which direction. Look around. Do your observations make sense? If so, are there any dangers nearby that would demand a more accurate estimate of your whereabouts? If not, are you satisfied that it is safe to continue on your way? Good. Proceed with caution.

Plotting a Dead Reckoning Position

If you are in any doubt about where you are, you should plot a *Dead Reckoning* (DR) *Position*. If no specific need has arisen, once an hour is a good rule of thumb.

The Estimated Position

Where there is tide, leeway and/or current, a DR must be adjusted to accommodate these factors. Doing so is a simple visual matter when proper plotting techniques are observed.

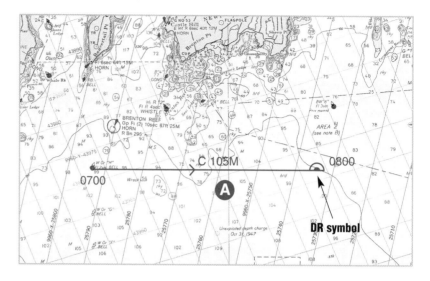

To establish a **DR position**, start from your last plotted position, then draw a line Ⓐ in the direction of the course steered. Its length is the logged distance run. Draw the DR symbol (see diagram) at its end and that is your Dead Reckoning Position. Label it with its time and note it in the ship's log if you are running one.

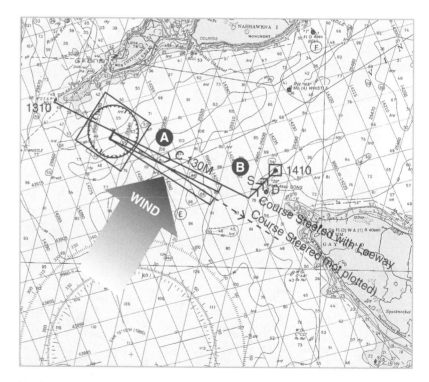

To plot an **estimated position**, start from your previous plotted position, then draw a line Ⓐ in the direction of the course steered. Its length is the logged distance from the previous plotted position. If there has been significant leeway, adjust it by rotating the plotter *downwind* to define the actual course you have made through the water. (Don't plot both lines.) Label this line as a course with a capital "C" (see page 68). Now draw in a tidal vector line Ⓑ at the end of the courseline (not at the departure point). Your EP is at the end of this line. It is marked by a square with a dot in the middle. Note the time against it and enter it in the ship's log if appropriate.

The Fix

Short of being situated immediately alongside a buoy or beacon, the "fix" is the nearest thing you can get to an absolutely sure position. It also allows you to check one source of information against another. It is usually more accurate than an EP, but without an EP (or at worst, an eyeball position) you will not know where to start looking for objects from which to deduce your fix. Also, there will be nothing to check your fix against to see if it is more or less in the right place.

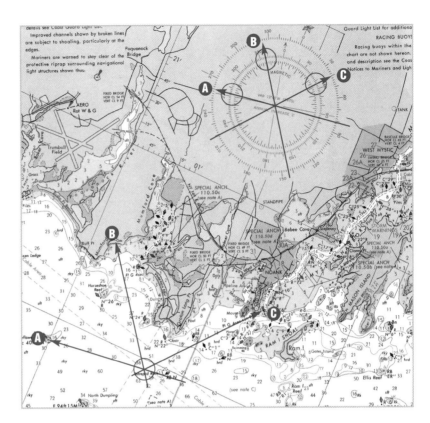

Plotting Symbols

085T	True heading
085M	Magnetic heading
085C	Compass heading
	DR position
	Estimated position
	"Conventional" fix
	Electronic fix
	Course to steer (or course steered)
	Course to steer corrected for leeway
	Track
	Current vector
	LOP

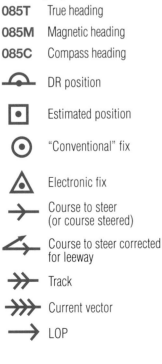

Your position is on the line **A** of your first bearing. To find out how far you are along it, take a bearing of a second object **B**. A bearing of a third object **C** will confirm that the cross of **A** and **B** is in the right place. The result is a triangle called a "cocked hat" with your fix somewhere inside it. Notice the plotting conventions. Label it with a time and note your log reading before entering the fix in the ship's log. If you are not using a ship's log, at least write the log reading against the fix, *because without a log reading, a fix is of no value as soon as you have sailed away from it.*

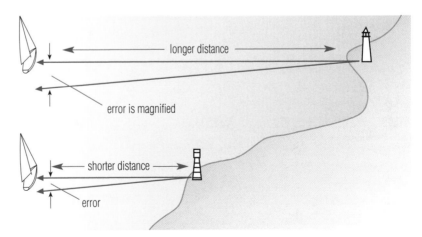

Choose your objects so the position lines (PLs) cross at a sensible angle. If they are too close together, a small error in bearing will give a large error in position. Always use a closer rather than a more distant object for an LOP when there is a choice. A small error in bearing is magnified with distance (see above).

The Ship's Log

The yacht's log book (always known as the *Ship's Log*) is the vital record from which all navigational deductions can be made. Any event of interest *must* be logged with at least a time and a log (distance) reading. You never know when you may need to refer back to it.

The ship's log must contain enough information to be able to work up a good EP from your last known position at any time. Make a log entry every time anything of significance occurs, but in any event, once an hour. If your electronics go down, the book will be all you have, so treat it with respect.

There are any number of things which you can enter in your ship's log and there many opinions about what columns should be available. The basics are shown below, however, and no boat should put to sea without them.

It is common practice among some U.S. navigators operating in conditions of extreme simplicity to work on the chart alone and not to run a ship's log. If this is your choice, *make sure that all positions have not only a time but also a log reading against them.* Failure to take this precaution will render all your efforts void, because without a log reading, you will not be able to work up your next EP or DR. A much better policy is to employ a simple ship's log ruled up yourself from an exercise book.

Note columns for *time, log, course, weather* and *remarks* in your log. *Engine hours* can also be useful. Some authorities believe there should be a column for latitude/longitude position if the yacht is equipped with electronics. Put one in if it makes you feel comfortable.

The courses and fixes for a passage from Camden Harbor are plotted on the chart and the accompanying log excerpts are shown below.

TIME	LOG	COURSE	WEATHER	REMARKS	ENGINE
0600	0	176 C	N3 1005 mb. Fair	Weighed anchor from Camden Harbor	30 mins.
0630	2.0	194 C	N2 1005 mb. Cloudy	G7 buoy at hand. Alter course to 194 C.	
0700	4.3	194 C	"	Fix taken on Lowell Rock light, Glen Cove Tower and Graves buoy. EP on chart.	
0750	8.2	163 C	"	G3 buoy at hand. Alter course to 163 C.	
0800	8.9	163 C	N2 1004 mb. Fog	Display radar reflector.	
0900	13.3	163 C	N2 1003 mb. Fog	EP and GPS fix on chart.	

Electronic Fixing Aids

Modern electronics have led to the general availability of a number of aids for helping to fix a yacht's position extremely accurately. Two systems are in general use:

GPS (Global Positioning System) takes its electronic PLs (position lines) from radio signals emitted by dedicated satellites. It is very accurate and is not subject to the errors common to terrestrial systems. It is, however, operated by the US Department of Defense, and may be switched off in times of crisis.

For more information on navigation, see US SAILING's Coastal Navigation and Passage Making.

Photo courtesy of *Northstar*

Loran C works on radio signals from terrestrial stations. It is subject to certain fixed errors and to uncertain variable ones. Plotting fixed errors is not always easy, but Loran has repeatable accuracy, meaning that a position given today will, even if in slight error, be given as the same one tomorrow. Variable errors are likely to occur at dawn, sunset, and during thunderstorms. Treat fixes with caution at these times.

Photo courtesy of Raytheon

A workable system of plotting latitude/longitude (lat/long) fixes is to use your **plotter or parallel rulers** for one coordinate, while employing dividers to supply the other. Once plotted, take a second look to *ensure* that it makes sense. ▼

In both Loran C and GPS systems, positions are read out as Latitude and Longitude. Plotting them requires systematic care and must always be double-checked. More strandings are caused by skippers who think they know where they are than ever result from honest doubt.

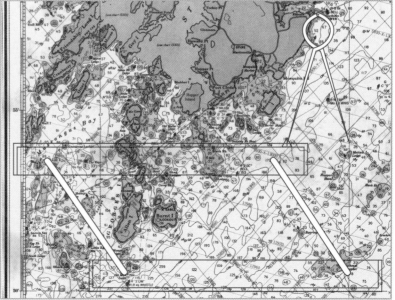

Inshore Pilotage

Inshore pilotage is the art of short-range navigating when things are happening too fast for formal chartwork. The techniques work by pre-planning a series of unmistakable straight-line routes from one safe place to the next. Sometimes you will find a pilot book useful. Occasionally you will have to work it out yourself. This page shows some favorite techniques.

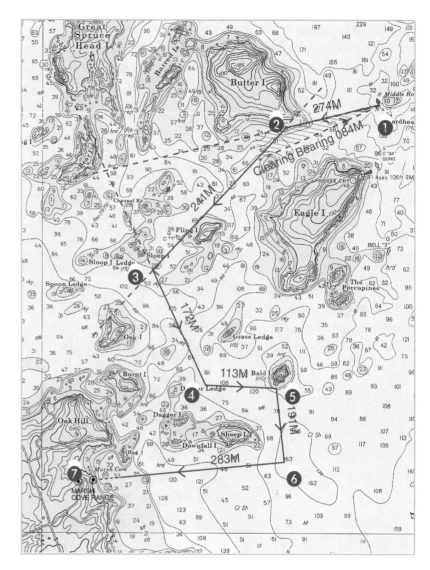

❶ From *Middle Rock* buoy, steer 274 M, keeping on track by heading for the house on *Bear Island* or watching a *back bearing* on the buoy. If it drifts off 094 M, you must correct accordingly. Keep checking your back bearing and whatever happens don't let it drop below 084 M as this *clearing bearing* (also called *danger bearing*) "clears" the submerged rocks north of *Eagle Island*.

As soon as C "1" off *Fling Island* bears 241 M, swing to port toward it ❷. You have only your compass to help you here, so it will be useful to line up the buoy on this bearing with a handy reference like an uncharted house on the right-hand side (RHS) of *Oak Island* or a rock that shows at low tide, then use this as an unofficial range. Once the range is organized, the compass is redundant and any cross set has been

neutralized. Once past the buoy, a back range can be formed between the can and the RHS of *Butter Island*.

Just after you have come abeam of *Sloop Island* and it lines up with the high hill on the left-hand side (LHS) of *Great Spruce Head Island*, you can proceed down this *natural range* steering 172 M ❸. If you don't like the looks of the rocks between *Dagger Island* and *Oak Hill*, you can swing to port when the RHS of *Bald Island* bears 111 M ❹ and steer a couple of degrees off the point at 113 M.

At *Bald Island*, come to starboard and steer 191 M ❺ which can be checked with a back bearing of 011 M. Leave *Sheep Island* to starboard and come onto the "official" *Marsh Cove Range* on 283 M ❻. As the depth shoals toward the 3-fathom contour, you can swing to starboard and anchor ❼.

Tropical Eyeball Pilotage

Always check your chart and sailing directions first. Having done so, the eyeball can be your best friend in clear water, particularly in the tropics. Do not expect great things early and late in the day. A high sun is an important part of the package, as is a good pair of polarized sunglasses.

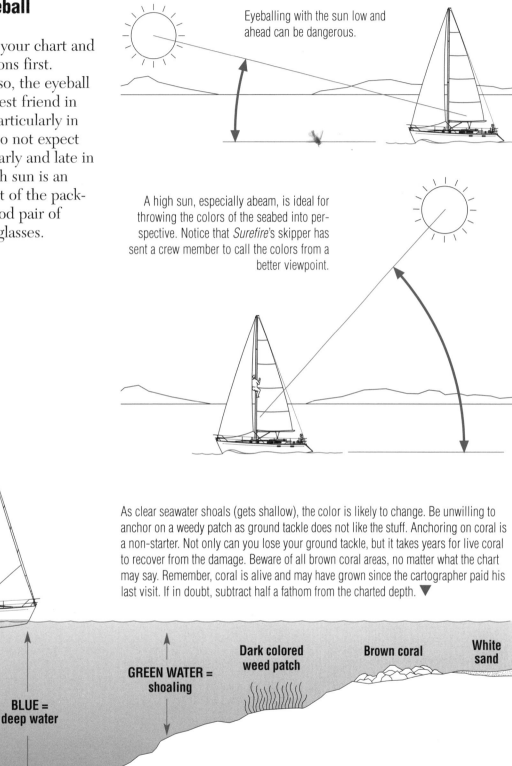

Eyeballing with the sun low and ahead can be dangerous.

A high sun, especially abeam, is ideal for throwing the colors of the seabed into perspective. Notice that *Surefire*'s skipper has sent a crew member to call the colors from a better viewpoint.

As clear seawater shoals (gets shallow), the color is likely to change. Be unwilling to anchor on a weedy patch as ground tackle does not like the stuff. Anchoring on coral is a non-starter. Not only can you lose your ground tackle, but it takes years for live coral to recover from the damage. Beware of all brown coral areas, no matter what the chart may say. Remember, coral is alive and may have grown since the cartographer paid his last visit. If in doubt, subtract half a fathom from the charted depth. ▼

BLUE = deep water

GREEN WATER = shoaling

Dark colored weed patch

Brown coral

White sand

Fog and Poor Visibility

Your first action when you see fog developing is to fix your position. Even if you have electronics this may be the last chance you'll get to reassure yourself that the computer is functioning as it should.

If you can't produce a fix, work up an EP as accurately as you can.

Safety Action to be taken:
▶ Double the look-out
▶ Hoist the radar reflector
▶ Listen hard for sound signals and other vessels
▶ Set a radar watch if appropriate
▶ Everyone on board should wear PFDs in case of collision.
▶ Sound fog signal

Sound Signals (every 2 minutes):
▶ under sail: ▬▬▬ ▬ ▬
  (prolonged, short, short)

▶ under power: ▬▬▬
  (prolonged)

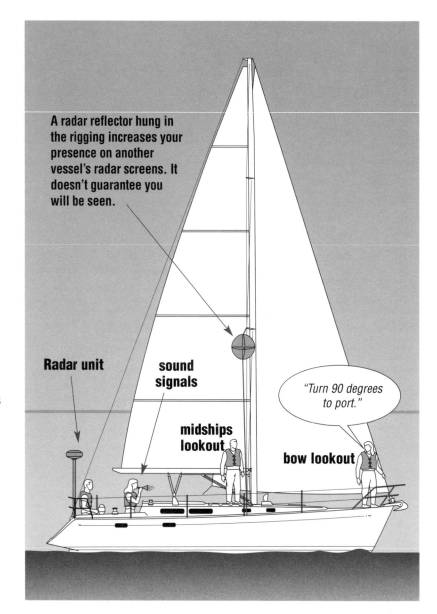

A radar reflector hung in the rigging increases your presence on another vessel's radar screens. It doesn't guarantee you will be seen.

Radar unit

sound signals

midships lookout

"Turn 90 degrees to port."

bow lookout

Radar Use
Radar is undoubtedly the best single electronic aid to navigation during reduced visibility, but interpreting the screen requires skill and experience. If you haven't taken a radar course, read the instruction manual for your set and practice using it in good weather, relating the picture to what you can see. Waiting for the fog to come down before using radar for the first time is a dangerous policy.

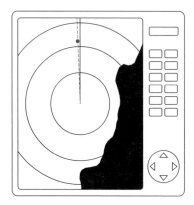

Some objects such as smaller fiberglass vessels will only show a return at close range. Change the range setting frequently.

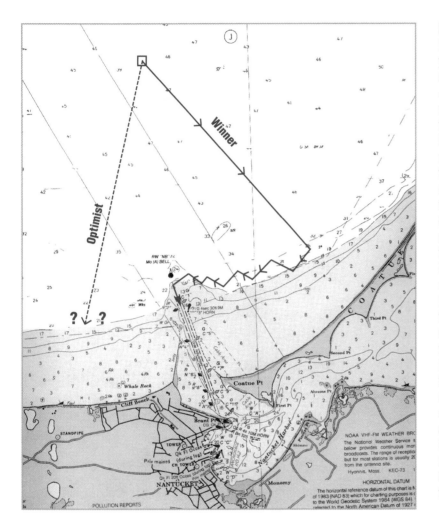

Running the Contour

If you are out at sea and lose sight of your landfall, do not tumble into the same trap as *Optimist* (see left). *Optimist*'s navigator has attempted to make directly for the harbor entrance from an estimated position, but the boat has drifted away to one side. When the navigator finds soundings similar to those near the channel entrance, the question remains, "Which way must I turn to find safe haven?" *Optimist* cannot know the answer and now has three diffi-cult options: 1) anchor, 2) go back out to sea from an unknown position, or 3) hope to get lucky and hear the horn. If not, *Optimist* can only turn arbitrarily to look for the entrance. *Winner* had done the right thing by opting to "miss" the entrance for certain to the left, knowing that when the boat finds 24 feet of water, it has only to turn to starboard and keep the depth at that figure by working in and out across the contour line until she comes to the bell buoy. Then *Winner* will also be hearing the horn. Once at the bell, they can turn in and steer down the right hand edge of the buoyed channel, keeping an eye on the depth to confirm their location.

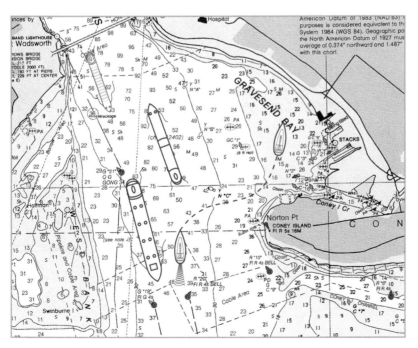

Playing it Safe

If you cannot make a safe harbor and there is heavy traffic around, you have two options: either sail far out to sea and heave-to or, preferably, make for shoal waters inshore and anchor in an area so shallow that a commercial ship could not hit you.

Hypothermia, Seasickness and Heat Emergencies

Sailing can expose you to extreme conditions, both hot and cold. On hot windless days, you'll be exposed to a lot of sun. On windy, overcast days, the cool spray coming over the bow can send a chill down your spine. Be prepared for these changes. Drink lots of water and wear clothing that protects your skin and head from the sun. Have warm clothing along in case the weather turns foul. Put on your jacket or pants before you get cold. In addition, you should know the warning signals for heat and cold emergencies and what to do in those situations.

SEASICKNESS

Sailing can cause motion sickness. You can reduce your chances of becoming seasick by getting plenty of sleep the night before you go sailing.
- Eat before going out, but avoid greasy, heavy foods and alcohol.
- Dress warmly.
- Some people use wrist bands that activate accupressure points. Others rely on prescription medications such as Scopolamine.
- Symptoms include yawning, burping, paleness, a headache or nausea . Get on deck for fresh air and watch the horizon to calm your sensory system. Better yet, steer the boat. Eating salted crackers or drinking a carbonated cola drink might help. In really bad cases, lie on your back in a spot where you're sheltered from cold and spray.

HYPOTHERMIA

SIGNALS...
- Shivering
- Impaired judgment
- Dizziness
- Numbness
- Change in level of consciousness
- Weakness
- Glassy stare

(Physical symptoms may vary, since age, body size, and clothing will cause individual differences.)

TREATMENT...
Medical assistance should be given to anyone with hypothermia. Until medical assistance arrives, these steps should be taken:
- Check breathing and pulse.
- Gently move the person to a warm place.
- Carefully remove all wet clothing. Gradually warm the person by wrapping in blankets or putting on dry clothes. Do not warm a person too quickly, such as immersing in warm water. Rapid rewarming may cause dangerous heart rhythms. Hot water bottles and chemical heat packs may be used if first wrapped in a towel or blanket before applying.
- Give warm, nonalcoholic and decaffeinated liquids to a conscious person only.

HEAT EXHAUSTION

SIGNALS...
- Cool, moist, pale skin
- Heavy sweating
- Headache
- Dizziness
- Nausea
- Weakness, exhaustion

TREATMENT...
Without prompt care, heat exhaustion can advance to a more serious condition — heat stroke. First aid includes:
- Move person to cool environment.
- Remove clothing soaked with perspiration and loosen any tight clothing.
- Apply cool, wet towels or sheets.
- Fan the person.
- Give person a half glass (4 oz.) of cool water every 15 minutes.

HEAT STROKE

SIGNALS...
- Red, hot, dry or moist skin
- Very high skin temperature
- Changes in level of consciousness
- Vomiting
- Rapid, weak pulse
- Rapid, shallow breathing

TREATMENT...
Heat stroke is life threatening. Anyone suffering from heat stroke needs to be cooled and an EMS technician should be contacted immediately. To care for heat stroke:
- Move person to cool environment.
- Apply cool, wet towels or sheets.
- If available, place ice or cold packs on the person's wrists and ankles, groin, each armpit, and neck.
- If unconscious, check breathing and pulse.

NOTE: First Aid and CPR classes are available nationwide. US SAILING recommends you attend one.

Treating Stove & Rope Burns and Sunburn

If you sustain a burn that doesn't break the skin, cover the wound with a cool, damp cloth to soothe and reduce pain. Follow the same procedure for a burn that breaks the skin, but seek medical assistance immediately. Keep the victim quiet and comfortable. Don't apply grease, oil or gooey substances to the affected area and do not attempt to break the blisters.

Do's & Don'ts

▶ Do disclose health issues such as medical problems, medications, allergic reactions, or pregnancy in advance to the captain and, if willing, others on board.

▶ Do check out First Aid kit before leaving charter dock.

CHARTERING SMART...

If you are allergic to bee stings, you are likely to be allergic to jellyfish stings. Consult your physician before setting sail.

FIRST AID CHECKLIST

▶ **FOOD POISONING** - Contaminated, improperly cooked or stored meat, fish and poultry, as well as unwashed fruits and vegetables, can cause violent cramps, nausea, vomiting and diarrhea. Seek professional assistance. With severe vomiting, don't force food or liquids. As soon as practical, have the victim take small amounts of water, rehydration drinks or other non-alcoholic liquids. The victim should rest quietly for 24 hours, consuming only liquids and small quantities of soft food such as salted crackers or boiled rice. Severe or prolonged diarrhea or vomiting causes dehydration and requires professional treatment. Ask your charter agent about freshly caught seafood and fish that may be poisonous.

▶ **DIARRHEA** - Unfamiliar foods and situations can cause diarrhea. Prevent dehydration by drinking water, rehydration drinks, or other non-alcoholic liquids. Avoid activity and stay out of the sun. If diarrhea persists, get medical assistance.

▶ **DEHYDRATION** - Drink plenty of water and other non-alcoholic liquids to help your system adjust to warmer climates. Stay out of the sun as much as possible.

EMERGENCY PROCEDURES

▶ In the event of a **life-threatening accident**, immediately summon help on the VHF radio with a Mayday call, by sounding a horn to attract attention or by sending someone ashore in the dinghy.

▶ Ensure the victim has an open airway. If there are **no signs of breathing**, give mouth to mouth or mouth to nose resuscitation.

▶ Control **severe bleeding** by applying direct pressure to the wound or to the nearest accessible artery that carries the blood supply to the wound. Move the victim only if absolutely necessary for safety.

▶ For **treatment of shock**, elevate the victim's feet and get professional help ASAP. Loosen constrictive clothing. Provide shade if victim cannot be moved.

CORAL CUTS

▶ Clean coral cuts with hydrogen peroxide and treat immediately with antibiotic cream. Beware of infection. If the cut becomes red, continue with the antibiotic cream. Reduce swelling with ice. Seek medical assistance if healing doesn't occur or red streaking appears around the wound.

Staying on Board

Recovering a victim that has fallen overboard is a four stage procedure:

1. re-gaining physical contact,
2. attaching to the boat,
3. getting back aboard and
4. aftercare.

Expertise in one without the others may prove deadly.

When going forward, always remember the maxim, "One hand for the boat, and one for yourself."

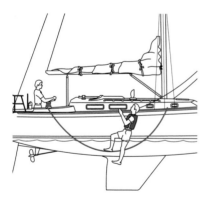

Make sure you try numerous methods of lifting overboard victims back on board, and see what else you can invent!

1) Regaining contact. As long as there are sailors there will be discussion about how best to regain contact with a victim, but a number of methods are broadly accepted.

2) Attaching the victim to the boat. A weak link in overboard recoveries is what happens after contact has been made. Victims holding onto a line have been known to let it slip out of their grasp as they succumb to fatigue and hypothermia. Take immediate action to attach the victim to the boat by clipping a line to the victim's harness or using a sling. Once attached to the boat, the victim can be recovered on board without fear of losing him or her. If recovery has been made with a Lifesling, properly clipped around the chest, this eliminates the problem.

3) Getting back aboard. Except in calm conditions, lifting a victim aboard can be far from easy. It must be borne in mind that there will certainly be some degree of shock, an injury may have been sustained and hypothermia may be setting in.

Boarding by ladder. If the swim ladder is mounted over the stern, be careful lest the boat's pitching causes the ladder or hull to injure the victim. Consider other means if this possibility seems real. In the case of a simple trip over the rails on a calm afternoon, however, the stern ladder is your first and obvious way.

Lifting by sling. The over-riding advantage of the Lifesling is that the victim is ready for a lift when brought alongside. You have only to hook up a spare halyard, lead it to a winch (ideally via a tackle kept for this purpose) and heave away, keeping a spare crew member (if you have one) standing by to assist the casualty. Unfortunately, this may well involve lifting the person vertically by the shoulders with the attendant dangers entailed. Try to raise the legs horizontally as soon as you can, and don't forget that if you cut your lifeline lanyards you have only to lift as far as the toe-rail. This method of lifting is also appropriate for use without a Lifesling, and some boats carry a simple under-arm "sling" for this purpose. Another system is to use the bosun's chair lowered into the water so that the casualty can work into it. There is a nasty moment in the early stages until the legs are out from under the boat, but thereafter the "bosun's lift" goes smoothly.

Other methods of getting the victim aboard. Often a victim can climb into the dinghy and then get aboard. An injured overboard victim assisted by a swimmer on a safety line can be floated into a half-inflated dinghy, so long as the yacht is laid across the wind to supply a lee. From here, they may be maneuvered round to a "sugar-scoop" stern, or rolled in under the lifelines. If the victim has been hit by the boom, be aware of the possibility that there may be a neck or spine injury and take the necessary precautions to try to avoid paralysis.

It cannot be over-stressed that the only way of achieving any degree of confidence that any of these systems will work, is to try them out. Practice with a wet-suited volunteer on a gentle day.

4) Aftercare. Take the greatest care of overboard victims who often succumb to hypothermia (refer to US SAILING's *Safety Recommendations for Cruising Sailboats* for further information on prevention, symptoms and treatment). Warm them gently with sleeping bags if cold, keep them lying down if the affair has been at all traumatic, and generally treat them like shock cases. If you are in any doubt at all or there is a suspicion of internal injuries, shock or water in the lungs, call up a "PAN-PAN medico" and ask for advice.

GOING FORWARD

► Wear footwear with good traction.
► When going forward it is safer to do so on the windward side.
► Lifelines work best if you keep your body low.
► Any openings in the rails of the bow or stern pulpit or lifelines should be securely closed while underway.
► Remember the maxim - "One hand for the boat and one for yourself".

One of the primary advantages of the Lifesling system is its ability to raise the victim back on board with a built-in block and tackle once the victim has been recovered.

Lifesling is deployed.

Victim is attached.

Victim is hoisted on board.

Quick-Stop Recovery

The hallmark of the Quick-Stop recovery method is the immediate reduction of boat speed by turning to windward and thereafter maneuvering at modest speed, remaining near the victim. Many consider this method superior to the conventional procedure of reaching off, then either jibing or tacking and returning on a reciprocal course, since the victim is kept in sight throughout. The Quick-Stop requires a tack and a jibe; and jibing in heavy weather conditions may be difficult for some boats and crews. It is generally regarded as a good method for short-handed sailing. Here are the steps:

1 Shout "Crew Overboard!" and provide immediate flotation for the victim. Throw buoyant objects such as cockpit cushions, life rings and so on as soon as possible. Even if these objects do not come to the aid of the victim, they will "litter the water" where he or she went overboard and help your spotter to keep the victim in view. Deployment of the overboard pole and flag (dan-buoy) requires too much time. The pole should be saved to "put on top" of the victim in case the initial maneuver is unsuccessful.

2 Designate a crew member to spot and point to the victim in the water. The spotter should NEVER take his or her eyes off the victim.

3 Bring the boat head-to-wind and beyond, leaving the headsail backed. If the overboard occurred off the wind, trim mainsail and headsail to close-hauled as the boat heads up. Keep turning with the headsail backed to further slow the boat until the wind is slightly abaft the beam. Do not release the sheets.

4 Head on a beam-to-broad reach course (approximately 90 to 120 degrees off the wind) for two or three boat lengths, then change course to nearly dead downwind.

5 Drop or furl the headsail (if possible) while keeping the mainsail centered (or nearly so). If the headsail is dropped, the headsail sheets should be kept tight to keep them and the sail inside the lifelines.

6 Jibe when the victim is abeam or aft of abeam of the boat (timing of jibe depends on the boat's maneuverability and performance in existing wind and sea conditions).

7 Approach the victim on a close reach course, adjusting speed with the mainsail; or glide up into the wind as you would when picking up a mooring. The approach will depend on your boat's maneuverability, position after your jibe, wind and sea conditions and helmsman's ability.

8 Stop the boat alongside the victim and establish contact with a heaving line or other device. A rescue throw bag with 50 to 75 feet of light floating line can be thrown into the wind because the line is kept inside the bag and trails out as it sails to the victim.

9 Attach the victim to the boat.

10 Recover the victim on board.

Quick-Stop Recovery

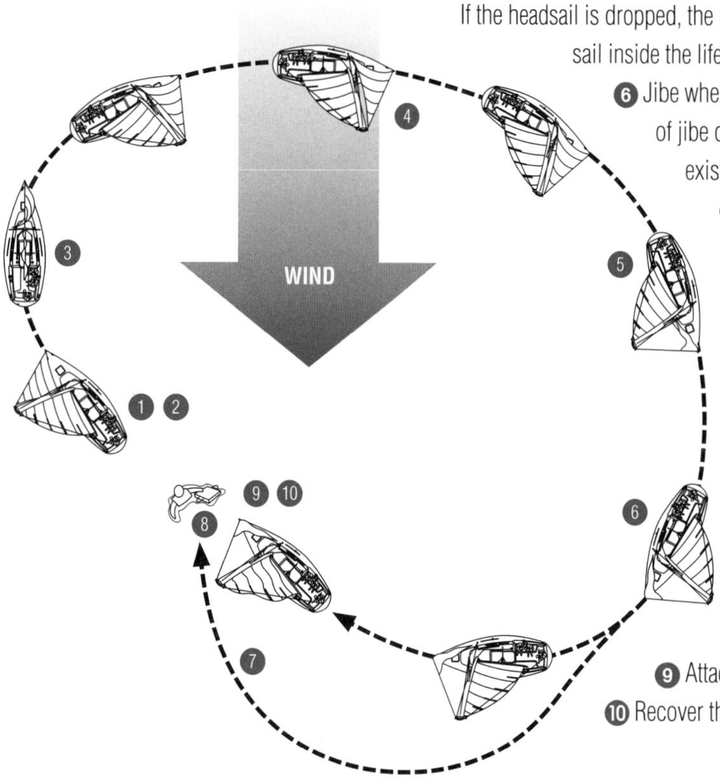

WIND

Lifesling-Type Recovery

If there are few people on board, the Lifesling-type recovery method should be employed. It takes longer than the Quick-Stop, but provides a means for a single crew member to effect a rescue of a victim in the water. This recovery requires these steps:

❶ As soon as a crew member falls overboard, throw a cushion or other buoyant objects to the victim and shout "Crew Overboard!" while the boat is brought IMMEDIATELY head-to-wind, slowed and stopped. The main is trimmed to centerline.

❷ The Lifesling is deployed by opening the bag that is hung on the stern pulpit and dropping the sling into the water. It will trail out astern and draw out the remaining line.

❸ Once the Lifesling is deployed, the boat is sailed in a wide circle around the victim with the line and sling trailing astern. The jib is not tended but allowed to back from the head-to-wind position, which increases the rate of turn.

❹ Contact is established with the victim by the line and sling being drawn inward by the boat's circling motion. The victim then places the sling over his or her head and under his or her arms.

❺ Upon contact, the boat is put head-to-wind again, the headsail is dropped to the deck or furled and the main is doused.

❻ As the boat drifts, the crew begins pulling the sling and the victim to the boat. If necessary, a cockpit winch can be used to assist in this phase, which should continue until the victim is alongside and pulled up tightly until he or she is suspended in the sling (so that he or she will not drop out).

This system is effective if: 1) line length is preadjusted to avoid running over the line, and 2) method is practiced to complete competence.

The Lifesling is a floating device attached to the boat by a length of floating line that doubles as a hoisting sling to retrieve a victim in the water. If the side of the boat is too high to reach the victim, or the victim is injured, the sling can be used to hoist the person up and over the lifelines.

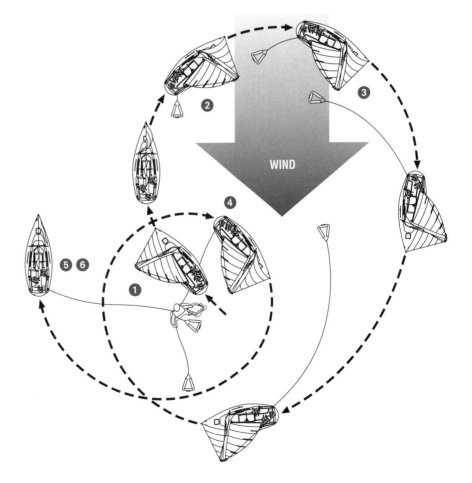

Quick-Turn Recovery

The Quick-Turn (or Figure-8) recovery avoids jibing during a recovery. In heavy weather, you may find controlling the boat easier with this recovery technique; *however, it is imperative to keep the victim in sight at all times!* Take the following steps in a Quick-Turn recovery:

① As soon as a crew member falls overboard, call out LOUDLY *"Crew overboard!"*

② Throw cushions, PFDs or life rings in the direction of the person in the water. Steer the boat on a beam reach.

③ Assign a crew member to watch and point at the person in the water. This crew member should NEVER take his or her eyes off the victim.

④ After sailing a maximum of four boatlengths, tack into the wind and fall off onto a deep broad reach, crossing the boat's original course.

⑤ When the victim is abeam of the boat, head up onto a close reach.

⑥ Ease sheets to slow the boat and bring it to a stop alongside the victim.

⑦ Attach the victim to the boat and recover on board.

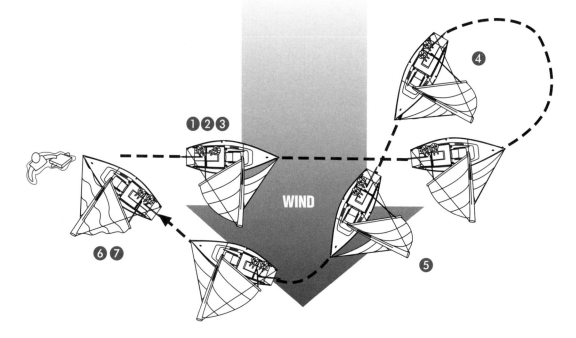

Recovery Under Power

In some situations, using your engine to recover a victim may be your only alternative.

① As soon as a crew member falls overboard, swing the propeller away from the victim, throw buoyant objects, such as cushions, PFDs or life rings, to the victim and shout "Crew Overboard!"

② Designate someone to spot and point at the person in the water. The spotter should NEVER take his or her eyes off the victim. Assign someone to make sure you're not trailing lines which could foul the prop.

③ Return to the victim. Side tie the dinghy to the boat to keep it clear as you maneuver.

④ Approach the victim with the boat headed into the wind at very slow speed, stop alongside the victim and shut off the engine.

⑤ Establish contact with the victim with a heaving line or other device.

⑥ Attach the victim to the boat and recover on board. Make sure neither the victim nor recovery device get near the propeller at any time during the maneuver. Be particularly alert using swim ladders and rear entry platforms.

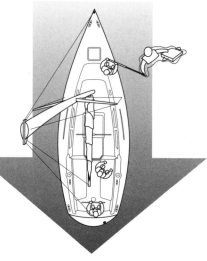

Heaving-to

Stopping the boat without anchoring is useful for lunch breaks and for coping with heavy weather. Steer close to the wind with the jib tightly sheeted. Tack, but don't release the jib. The boat will bear away from the wind on the new tack. To counteract the backed jib, put the helm over to steer the boat upwind, tighten the brake or tie the wheel and trim the mainsail so the boat lies almost close-hauled to the wind and waves. The boat will sail up to about 40 degrees to the wind and then come off to about 60 degrees, and then repeat the motion again. Always maintain a watch when you heave-to.

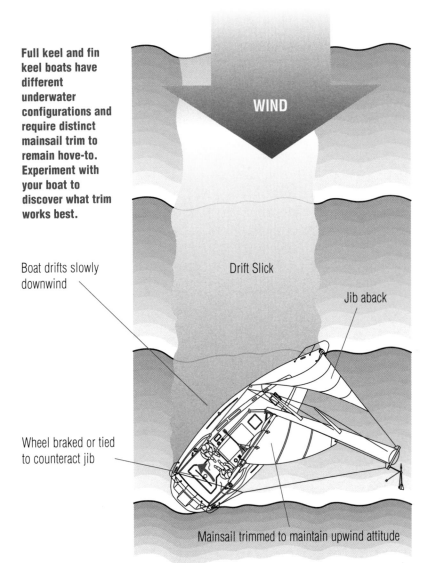

Full keel and fin keel boats have different underwater configurations and require distinct mainsail trim to remain hove-to. Experiment with your boat to discover what trim works best.

WIND

Drift Slick

Jib aback

Boat drifts slowly downwind

Wheel braked or tied to counteract jib

Mainsail trimmed to maintain upwind attitude

Engine Failure

Prepare for engine failure by thinking about how you would control the boat in situations where you might lose power. Your action plan should include at least three steps: assess the situation, ensure the safety of crew and maximize your response options.

Situation	Response
Open water	Set sails, heave-to or drift. Troubleshoot the engine.
Busy channel	Set sail or drift to edge of channel. Anchor clear of traffic. Intentional grounding in a safe area is a viable option.
Close quarters	Rig fenders and drift or sail to a dock, moor, anchor or raft to moored boat.
Lee shore	Anchor immediately. If anchoring is not feasible, raise jib to get way on. Be aware than many sailboats will not sail upwind under headsail alone.

Unfouling a Propeller

Fouling your propeller can frustrate you and can, in some situations, be perilous. To avoid serious damage to the engine or the propeller and shaft, stop the engine, shift to neutral and assess the situation. If you can't free the propeller, remember you can still sail the boat to your next destination. If you are in danger of drifting onto a lee shore, anchor the boat immediately and then attend to the propeller.

With a sharp knife or hacksaw, dive under the boat and cut away the fouled line. Diver should wear a safety line and beware of swells and currents.

A line trailing from the boat or a fish trap can wrap around the spinning shaft.

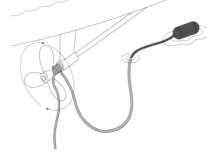

The propeller stops turning because the line jams the shaft in place. If your engine runs in neutral but stalls in gear, suspect a fouled shaft.

Crew on deck takes up slack as line unwinds.

Remove the bilge boards covering the shaft and rotate it by hand in the opposite of its last direction.

ACTION PLAN CHECKLIST

▶ Shift to neutral immediately.
▶ Anchor the boat if possible.
▶ Free the line from the shaft.
▶ Sail the boat.

Do's & Don'ts

▶ Do shift into neutral as soon as you detect a fouled propeller.
▶ Don't shift into reverse to attempt to free the line.
▶ Do shut down the engine while attempting to unfoul the propeller.
▶ Do ensure there is no load on the line while unfouling it.
▶ Don't restart your engine until the diver is back on board.
▶ Don't dive under the boat in rough water conditions.

Steering Failure

If you have a steering failure, the emergency tiller provides a back up. Know where it's stowed and practice installing it before leaving the dock. Attaching the tiller may require removal of the wheel. If your steering quadrant or cable breaks while underway in open water, trim the sails to maintain your course while you complete the emergency installation.

Wheel
Turning the wheel turns the sprocket and chain which moves the steering cables.

Pedestal
Inside the pedestal, the wheel has a sprocket and chain to which the steering cables are attached.

Sheave
Check the sheaves for wearing or chafe by looking for signs of metal particles.

Emergency Tiller

Sheave
Each cable runs from the pedestal through a sheave under the cockpit sole.

Steering Cable
Check the cable for binding, fraying, tension and perfect alignment.

Rudder Post
The rudder post extends above the quadrant for the emergency tiller.

Quadrant
The quadrant connects the steering cables to the rudder post and turns in response to the pulling of the cables.

Remove the access plate above the top of the rudder post to install the emergency tiller. In this photo, the wheel has been removed to allow unobstructed movement of the tiller.

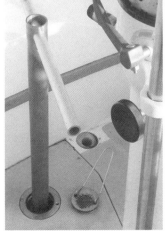

Running Aground

Running aground on a descending tide can be serious depending on the tidal range, the type of bottom, and the type of keel. If hard aground, use any combination of kedging, heeling and motoring to free your boat. If another boat can tow you off, use a strong line such as your anchor rode and attach it to a sturdy part of your boat, *not* around a deck-stepped mast! If you cannot free a vessel, set an anchor in deeper water and await the returning tide. Close all ports, hatches and lazarettes securely to prevent water from filling the boat as it refloats.

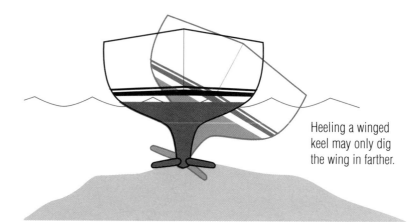

Heeling a winged keel may only dig the wing in farther.

Backing Off Under Power
If there's no damage to the boat or crew, attempt to back off under power keeping the rudder straight.

ACTION PLAN CHECKLIST

▶ Make sure everyone is okay.
▶ Determine if the boat is damaged and check for leaks in the bilge.
▶ Try to back off in the direction you came from.

Heeling the Boat
You can decrease the boat's depth *(draft)* by heeling over. Swing the boom out to the side and have members of the crew sit on it. This may free the keel from the bottom. The main halyard should be used at the end of the boom to reinforce the topping lift.

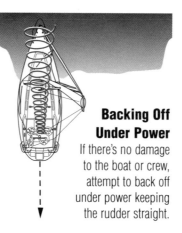

Kedging
Using your anchor, you can also pull yourself free *(kedge off)*. Use your dinghy to carry the anchor directly astern until you reach a scope of about 5:1. Lead the anchor line to a cockpit sheet winch and grind the line in with the rudder straight. (If there's no dinghy, float the anchor with PFDs and swim it out.)

Squalls and Storms

Blackening and growing clouds, especially in the tropics, usually indicate short-term storms called squalls. If you are close to a harbor of refuge, a short motorsail to a protected area may be the best solution. If obstructions are close by or the only safe harbor is some distance to windward, sail toward deeper water. Prepare for the worst by reefing, changing to smaller sails or heaving-to in adequate sea room. Sailing off the wind reduces the strain on the boat.

Defined groups of dark clouds often bring squalls, which may include strong wind or heavy rain or both. Only infrequently do these clouds pass without incident.

Stock Newport photo

Roll the furling headsail tightly and wrap the jib sheets around the sail. Tension jib sheets and cleat them.

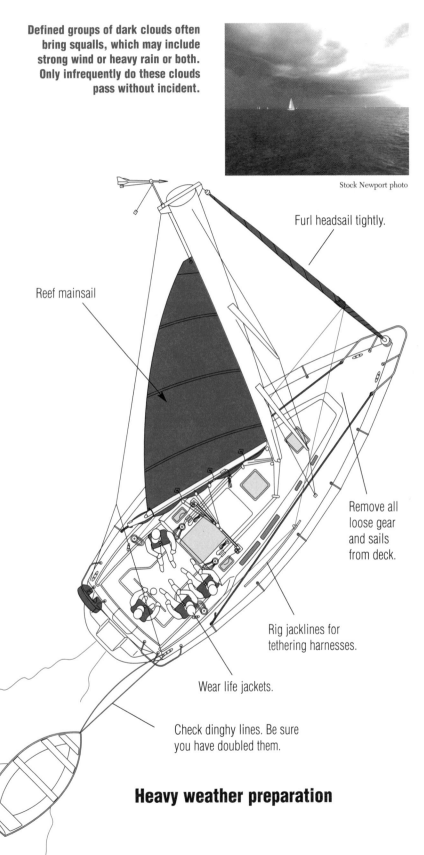

Furl headsail tightly.

Reef mainsail

Remove all loose gear and sails from deck.

Rig jacklines for tethering harnesses.

Wear life jackets.

Check dinghy lines. Be sure you have doubled them.

Heavy weather preparation

Flooding

Deal quickly with water in the boat. Make sure everyone puts on a PFD. The most experienced crew should check the source of flooding. Everyone else should pump the bilge or bail with buckets. If the leak wasn't caused by collision, taste the water to see whether it's fresh or salt. One of the first things to check are the head valves. Then look for leaking hoses, a broken through-hull fitting, a leak in the water tank, an overflow from the shower sump, an open hatch, or a leaky stuffing box. If you've been holed, heel the boat to attempt to elevate the opening above the waterline. Plug the hole or at least try to slow the rate of flooding. If you can't keep up with the water flow, put out a Mayday call.

If available, ease a small sail over the bow with control lines tied on each corner. Water pressure will move the sail aft to the damaged area. Carefully work the sail around the keel and secure control lines. From the inside, plug the hole with sailbags, cushions or seabags held down by a door or sole board wedged in by a whisker pole or mop handles. If interior liner is not holed you may have to destroy it to expose the hole.

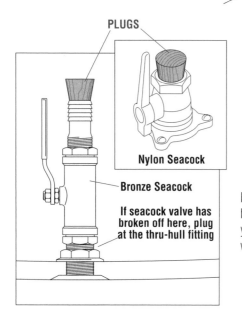

PLUGS

Nylon Seacock

Bronze Seacock

If seacock valve has broken off here, plug at the thru-hull fitting

Flooding may happen if a through-hull fitting breaks, in which case you should pound the designated wooden plug into the hole.

Do's & Don'ts

▶ Do think through alternatives for saving the crew and the boat.

▶ Don't abandon ship unless there are NO other alternatives.

▶ Do maneuver the boat to shallow water or a safe harbor. Intentionally grounding the boat may be the safest way to save the crew and later the boat.

▶ Don't use a Mayday unless you are in a life-threatening situation. Use Pan-Pan instead.

▶ Do follow charter company procedures.

Sinking

Abandon ship *only* if your boat is sinking and you have no alternatives. A small raft is much harder to find at sea than a boat. If a vessel is not already standing by, issue a Mayday call, giving your location and number of crew. If your boat has no liferaft, you will have to use the dinghy. Attempt to keep crew and gear as dry as possible when transferring from boat.

ACTION PLAN CHECKLIST

► Notify everyone that it's time to abandon ship and make sure they are wearing warm clothes and a PFD.
► Assign each crew a specific task:
  • tying the liferaft to a structural part of the boat and deploying it overboard
  • activating the EPIRB
  • sending Mayday on VHF radio per page 27
  • firing flares
  • getting food and water
► Take EPIRB, handheld VHF radio with you.
► Get into raft.
► Cut painter when everyone is accounted for.

Distress Signals

Flares fired from a pistol or launcher are visible over the horizon day or night. Handheld flares can pinpoint your location for rescuers, but should be used with great caution around a rubber raft. The U.S. Coast Guard requires vessels over 16 feet to have three daylight and three night flares or three combination daylight/night devices readily available, which have not expired. Sound horns and bells continuously. Use flashlight or radio to send the international SOS ($\cdots — — — \cdots$).

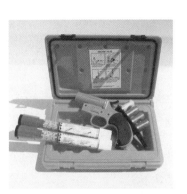

The Emergency Position-Indicating Radio Beacon (EPIRB) issues a signal to satellites and aircraft when activated. Use only in extreme emergencies.

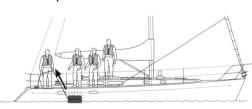

Deploying a Liferaft

❶ Tie off painter to structural part of boat. Keep knife handy to cut painter, if necessary.

❷ Have the strongest crew member push or throw canister or satchel into the water.

❸ Pull out painter to activate CO2 inflation.

❹ Do not leave until the boat is so low that you have to step UP into the liferaft.

Going Aloft

Some maintenance chores, such as checking the rigging or changing a light bulb, require going aloft. If possible, go up the mast in smooth water conditions and always observe safety precautions.

Don't entrust your life to the halyard shackle alone. Tape the shackle shut and tie an extra line or sail tie through the halyard thimble to the harness rings.

GOING ALOFT CHECKLIST

- ▶ Tie a safety line through the halyard thimble to the harness rings.
- ▶ Rig a second halyard, if available, as a safety.
- ▶ Stand away from the mast while crew is aloft.
- ▶ Use a horn cleat for making halyard fast.
- ▶ Cleat halyard while crew works aloft.
- ▶ Lower crew steadily and smoothly. Slow down to pass spreaders and shrouds.
- ▶ Send tools and spares up in a bucket or bag, or tie to the bosun's chair.

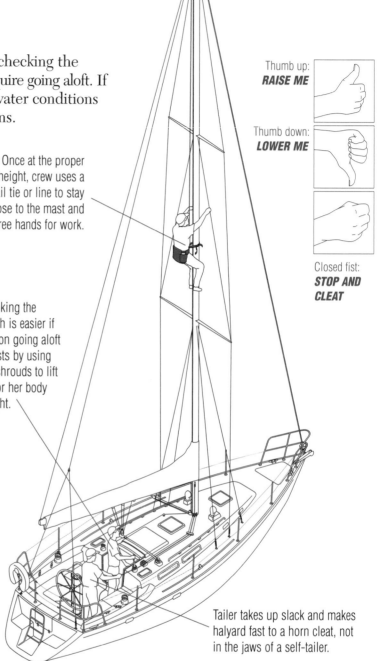

Thumb up:
RAISE ME

Thumb down:
LOWER ME

Closed fist:
STOP AND CLEAT

Once at the proper height, crew uses a sail tie or line to stay close to the mast and to free hands for work.

Cranking the winch is easier if person going aloft assists by using the shrouds to lift his or her body weight.

Tailer takes up slack and makes halyard fast to a horn cleat, not in the jaws of a self-tailer.

When lowering a crew member, have enough wraps on the winch drum and use the palm of your hand on the wraps to control the descent. At the same time, avoid too many wraps, which can lead to overrides and jams.

Troubleshooting

The best maintained boat still has bad days. If you are prepared to handle the very common problems that occur in boat systems, you will be a more independent cruiser.

ENGINE

1 If the engine overheats and the alternator doesn't charge, check the alternator and raw-water pump belts for tight fit.

2 If the engine overheats, check the exhaust for water. Make sure the raw-water intake is open and clear, and the raw-water filter is clean.

3 If the oil in the engine looks like chocolate milk, water is getting into the engine. Call a mechanic.

4 If the engine turns over but won't run, make sure the engine stop control is in the RUN position or fuel won't reach the engine. Check the fuel filter for debris and make sure the fuel tank valve is open.

5 If engine alarm sounds while running under power, check temperature and oil pressure gauges/lights and stop the engine.

6 If the engine exhaust water stops, one of the first things to check is the raw-water filter.

7 If the control cables break, the controls can be operated from the engine.

8 If you smell diesel exhaust in the cabin, check to see if there's a hole in the exhaust system. Let the engine cool and cover the hole with a piece of aluminum can and hose clamps.

STEERING

1 If it's hard to turn the wheel, see if the wheel brake is set too tightly.

2 If you see metal filings under the steering sheaves or quadrant, check for a binding cable.

3 If the steering wheel feels unresponsive, make sure the cable is tight and hasn't jumped the quadrant.

4 If the steering cable breaks, use the emergency tiller on the rudder post.

ELECTRICAL

1 If the batteries don't accept a charge, check the alternator belt and battery water level.

2 If the batteries discharge too quickly, check that the alternator belt is tight, the connections and terminals on the batteries are clean, the electrical usage is being monitored, and try charging them longer.

3 If the electrical system doesn't work, check the switches and fuses on the electrical control panel. Look for loose connections.

4 If the starting battery won't start the engine, turn the battery switch to ALL (BOTH).

HEAD AND FRESH WATER

1 If water doesn't pump into the bowl, check that the intake seacock and hand or foot lever are open.

2 If it is hard to pump, check the Y-valve and holding tank. It may be full.

3 If the head is clogged, close the seacocks and disconnect the hoses. Beware that the hoses are under pressure. Protect the boat from the sewage and open wounds from infection. Check the Y-valve. Check the pump by taking it apart. Typically, the last person to use the head gets to unclog it.

4 A constantly running pressure water pump may indicate a leak in the system or an empty water tank that could burn out the pump.

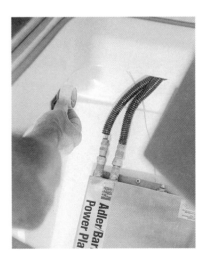

REFRIGERATION

1 If the unit runs continuously, open the unit less frequently.

2 If items don't stay cold or ice melts too soon, make sure the box is closed. Check the thermostat setting.

3 If the unit cools mechanically off the engine but doesn't stay cold, run the engine longer or more often.

Glossary of Sailing Terms

Including radio/signal flag terms (in parenthesis)

▶ A (Alfa)

Abeam - off the side of (at right angle to) the boat.

Aft - at or toward the stern or behind the boat.

Alternator - a device which generates electricity from an engine.

Amidships - toward the center of the boat.

Apparent wind - the wind aboard a moving boat.

Astern - behind the stern of the boat.

Athwartships - across the boat from side to side.

▶ B (Bravo)

Back - 1.- to hold the clew of a sail out to windward. 2.- a counterclockwise change of wind direction.

Back & fill - using forward and reverse gears, as well as an inboard engine's prop walk and rudder angles, to turn a boat in close quarters.

Backstay - the standing rigging running from the stern to the top of the mast.

Ballast - weight in the keel that provides stability.

Barometer - a weather forecasting instrument that measures air pressure.

Batten - a thin slat that slides into a pocket in the leech of a sail, helping it hold its shape.

Battery switch - the main electrical cutoff switch.

Beam - the width of a boat at its widest point.

Beam reach - (point of sail) sailing in a direction at approximately 90 degrees to the wind.

Bear away - to fall off, head away from the wind.

Bearing - the direction from one object to another expressed in compass degrees.

Beating - a course sailed upwind.

Below - the area of a boat beneath the deck.

Bend - to attach a sail to a spar or a headstay, or to attach a line to a sail.

Berth - 1. -the area in which you park your boat; 2. - the area in which you sleep on a boat.

Bight - a loop in a line.

Bilge - the lowest part of the boat's interior, where water on board will collect.

Bimini - a sun awning used to cover the cockpit area.

Bitter end - the end of a line.

Blanket - to use a sail or object to block the wind from filling a sail.

Block - a pulley on a boat.

Boat hook - a pole with a hook used for grabbing hold of a mooring or an object in the water.

Bolt rope - the rope sewn into the foot and luff of some mainsails and the luff of some jibs by which the sails are attached to the boat.

Boom vang - a block and tackle system which pulls the boom down to assist sail control.

Bow - the forward part of the boat.

Bow line (BOW - line) - a line running from the bow of the boat to the dock or mooring.

Bowline - (BOE-lin) - a knot designed to make a loop that will not slip and can be easily untied.

Breast line - a short dockline leading off the beam of the boat directly to the dock.

Broach - an uncontrolled rounding, usually from a downwind point of sail.

Broad reach - (point of sail) sailing in a direction with the wind at the rear corner of the boat (approximately 135 degrees from the bow).

Bulkhead - a wall that runs athwartships on a boat, usually providing structural support to the hull.

By the lee - sailing on a run with the wind coming over the same side of the boat as the boom.

▶ C (Charlie)

Cabin - the interior of a boat.

Can - an odd-numbered, green buoy marking the left side of a channel as you return to port.

Cast off - to release a line.

Centerline - the midline of a boat running from bow to stern.

Center of Effort - the focal point of the force of the wind on the sails.

Center of Lateral Resistance - the focal point of the force of the water on the underbody of the boat.

Chafe - wear on a line caused by rubbing.

Chainplates - strong metal plates which connect the shrouds to the boat.

Channel - a (usually narrow) path in the water, marked by buoys, in which the water is deep enough to sail.

Chart - a nautical map.

Charter - to rent a boat.

Chock - a guide mounted on the deck through which docklines and anchor rode are run.

Choke - a device for controlling the mixture of air and fuel for a gasoline engine.

Chop - rough, short, steep waves.

Clew - the lower, aft corner of a sail.

Close-hauled - the point of sail closest to the wind.

Close reach - (point of sail) sailing in a direction with the wind forward of the beam, but aft of the close-hauled position.

CNG - Compressed Natural Gas, a cooking fuel.

Coaming - the short wall surrounding the cockpit.

Cockpit - the lower area in which the steering controls and sail controls are located.

Coil - to loop a line neatly so it can be stored.

Come about - see **tack**.

Companionway - the steps leading from the cockpit or deck to the cabin below.

Compass - the magnetic instrument which indicates the

direction in which the boat is headed.

Compass protractor - a plotting instrument oriented to latitude-longitude lines.

Compass rose - the circle(s) on a chart which indicates the direction of true north and magnetic north.

Converter - a device to change AC current to DC.

Course - the direction in which the boat is steered.

Courtesy flag - the national flag of a host country.

Cowl - a ventilator funnel on deck.

Crew - besides the skipper, anyone on board.

Cringle - a ring sewn into the sail through which a line can be passed.

Cunningham - a line running through a grommet near the tack of a mainsail used to tighten the luff.

Current - the horizontal movement of water caused by tides, wind and other forces.

▶ D (Delta)

Dead downwind - sailing in a direction straight downwind.

Deck plate - a covered opening on deck leading to the water, fuel or holding tanks, or for access to the rudder post.

Depower - to release the power from the sails by allowing them to luff or making them flatter.

Dinghy - a small sailboat, rowboat or small boat with outboard.

Displacement - the weight of a boat; therefore the amount of water it displaces.

Divider - instrument used for measuring distances or coordinates on a chart.

Dock - 1. - the wooden structure where a boat may be tied up. 2. - the act of bringing the boat to rest alongside the structure.

Dockline - a line used to secure the boat to the dock.

Dodger - a canvas protection in front of the cockpit designed to keep spray off the skipper and crew.

Dog - 1. **-** screw type latches on ports. 2. - to fasten a port or hatch securely.

Dorade - a cowled box vent that prevents water from penetrating below decks.

Downhaul - a line used to pull down on the movable gooseneck to tighten the luff of the mainsail. The cunningham has the same function on other boats.

Downwind - away from the direction of the wind.

Draft - the depth of a boat from the water's surface.

▶ E (Echo)

Ease - to let out a line or sail.

Ebb - an outgoing tide.

EPIRB - Emergency Position-Indicating Radio Beacon

▶ F (Foxtrot)

Fairlead - a fitting that guides a jib sheet or other lines back to the cockpit or along the deck.

Fairway - the center of a channel.

Fake - to lay out a line on deck using large loops to keep it from becoming tangled.

Fall off - see **head down**.

Fast - secured.

Fathom - a measurement of the depth of water. One fathom equals six feet.

Feathering - sailing close to the wind to depower the sails.

Feathering propeller - a propeller with blades that align with the water flow.

Fender - a rubber bumper used to protect a boat.

Fetch - 1. - see **lay**. 2. - a distance of open water between a shore and a position over which waves build up.

Fishhooks - strands of frayed wire that can cut your skin or rip sails.

Fitting - a piece of nautical hardware.

Float plan - an itinerary of your intended sailing trip, left with a responsible party onshore.

Float switch - a device which turns on the bilge pump when water inside the boat reaches a certain height.

Flood - an incoming tide.

Flotilla - a group of boats on an organized cruise.

Following sea - waves hitting the boat from astern.

Foot - the bottom edge of a sail.

Fore - forward.

Forepeak - a storage area in the bow (below the deck).

Foresail - a jib or a genoa.

Forestay - the standing rigging running from the bow to the mast to which the jib is hanked on.

Forward - toward the bow.

Fouled - tangled.

Freeboard - the height of the hull above the water's surface.

Full - not luffing.

Furl - to fold or roll up a sail.

▶ G (Golf)

Genoa - a large jib whose clew extends aft of the mast.

Gimbal - a contrivance or system which keeps items horizontal as the boat heels.

Give-way vessel - the vessel required to change course when on a collision course with another boat.

Glide zone - the distance a sailboat takes to coast to a stop.

Gooseneck - the strong fitting that connects the boom to the mast.

Grommet - a reinforcing metal ring set in a sail.

Ground tackle - the anchor and rode (chain and line).

Gunwale (GUN-nle) - the edge of the deck where it meets the topsides.

▶ H (Hotel)

Halyard - a line used to hoist or lower a sail.

Hank - a snap hook that is used to connect the luff of a jib onto the forestay.

"Hard a-lee" - the command given to the crew just prior to tacking.

Hard over - to turn the tiller or wheel as far as possible in one direction.

Harness - see **safety harness**.

Hatch - a large covered opening in the deck.

Hatch boards - boards that close off the companionway.

Haul in - to tighten a line.

Head - 1. - the top corner of a sail. 2. - the bathroom on a boat. 3. - the toilet on a boat.

Headboard - the reinforcing small board affixed to the head of a sail.

Header - a wind shift which makes your boat head down or sails to be sheeted in.

Heading - the direction of the boat expressed in compass degrees.

Head down - to change course away from the wind.

Head off - see **head down**.

Head up - to change course toward the wind.

Headsail - a jib, genoa, or staysail.

Headstay - the standing rigging running from the bow to the mast.

Head-to-wind - the course of the boat when the bow is dead into the wind.

Headway - progress made forward.

Heave-to - to hold one's position in the water by using the force of the sails and rudder to counter one another.

Heavy weather - strong winds and large waves.

Heel - the lean of a boat caused by the wind.

Helm - the tiller or wheel.

Helmsman - the person responsible for steering the boat.

Holding ground - the bottom ground in an anchorage used to hold the anchor.

Holding tank - part of MSD system which allows storage of effluence rather than pumping it overboard.

Hove-to - a boat that has completed the process of heaving-to, with its jib aback, its main loosely trimmed, and its rudder securely positioned to steer it close to the wind.

Hull speed - the theoretical maximum speed of a sailboat determined by the length of its waterline.

▶ I (India)

Inboard - inside of the rail of a boat.

In irons - a boat that is head-to-wind, making no forward headway.

Inverter - a device to change DC current to AC.

Isobar - a line joining places of equal air pressure as depicted on weather maps.

▶ J (Juliet)

Jacklines - sturdy wire, rope or webbing securely fastened at its ends on deck which permits the crew to hook in with their safety harnesses.

Jib - the small forward sail attached to the forestay.

Jibe - to change direction of a boat by steering the stern through the wind.

"Jibe-ho" - the command given to the crew when starting a jibe.

Jiffy reef - a quick reefing system allowing a section of the mainsail to be tied to the boom.

Jury rig - an improvised, temporary repair.

▶ K (Kilo)

Kedge off - to use an anchor to pull a boat into deeper water after it has run aground.

Keel - the heavy vertical fin beneath a boat that helps keep it upright and prevents it from slipping sideways in the water.

Kill switch - engine stop control.

King spoke - a marker on the steering wheel which indicates when the rudder is centered.

Knockdown - a boat heeled so far that one of its spreaders touches the water.

Knot - one nautical mile per hour.

▶ L (Lima)

Land breeze - a wind blowing over land and out to sea.

Lash - to tie down.

Lay - to sail a course that will clear an obstacle without tacking.

Lazarette - a storage compartment built into the deck.

Lazy sheet - the windward side jib sheet that is not under strain.

Lead (LEED) - to pass a line through a fitting or block.

Lee helm - the boat's tendency to turn away from the wind.

Lee shore - land which is on the leeward side of the boat. Because the wind is blowing in that direction, a lee shore could pose a danger.

Leech - the after edge of a sail.

Leech line - an adjustable cord sewn into the back edge of a sail to prevent fluttering.

Leeward - (LEW-erd) - the direction away from the wind (where the wind is blowing to).

Leeward side - the side of the boat or sail that is away from the wind.

Leeway - sideways slippage of the boat in a direction away from the wind.

Lifeline - plastic coated wire, supported by stanchions, around the outside of the deck to help prevent crew members from falling overboard.

Lifesling - a floating device attached to the boat by a length of floating line that doubles as a hoisting sling to retrieve a victim in the water.

Lift - 1. - the force that results from air passing by a sail, or water past a keel, that moves the boat forward and sideways. 2. - a change in wind direction which lets the boat head up.

Line - a nautical rope.

Line stoppers - levered cleats which hold lines under load and can be released easily.

Lubber's line - a small post in a compass used to help determine a course or a bearing.

Luff - 1. - the forward edge of a sail. 2. - the fluttering of a sail caused by aiming too close to the wind.

▶ M (Mike)

Magnetic - in reference to magnetic north rather than true north.

Mainmast - the tallest mast on a boat.

Marlinspike - a pointed tool used to loosen knots.

Master switch - see **battery switch**.

Masthead - the top of the mast.

Masthead fly - a wind direction indicator on top of the mast.

Mast step - the structure that the bottom of the mast sits on.

Mayday - the internationally recognized distress signal for a life-threatening emergency.

Mooring - a permanently anchored ball or buoy to which a boat can be tied.

MSD - marine sanitation device, including toilet, holding tank and connecting lines and valves.

▶ N (November)

Nautical mile - a distance of 6076 feet, equaling one minute of the earth's latitude.

Navigation Rules - laws established to prevent collisions on the water.

No-Go Zone - an area into the wind in which a boat cannot produce power to sail.

Nun - a red, even-numbered buoy, marking the right side of a channel as you return to port. Nuns are usually paired with cans.

▶ O (Oscar)

Offshore - away from or out of sight of land.

Offshore wind - wind blowing away from the land.

Off the wind - sailing downwind.

On the wind - sailing upwind, close-hauled.

Outboard - 1. - a portable engine with propeller mounted on the transom. 2. - a position away from the centerline of the boat.

Outhaul - the controlling line attached to the clew of a main-sail used to tension the foot of the sail.

Overpowered - a boat that is heeling too far because it has too much sail up for the amount of wind.

Overtaking - a boat that is catching up to another boat and about to pass it.

▶ P (Papa)

Packing gland - see **stuffing box**.

Painter - the line attached to the bow of a dinghy.

Pan-Pan - the internationally recognized distress signal for an urgent, but not life-threatening, situation.

Parallel rulers - two rulers linked and held parallel by hinges used to plot a course.

Pasarelle - used in Med Mooring, a plank or gangway connecting transom to dock or quay.

Pay out - to ease a line.

Pennant - added length of wire or line used on mooring buoys, also used on sails to lengthen hoist.

PFD - abbreviation for Personal Flotation Device; a life jacket.

Piling - vertical timber or log driven into the sea bottom to support docks or form a breakwater.

Pinching - sailing too close to the wind.

Plot - applying calculations to a chart to determine course or position.

Point - to steer close to the wind.

Points of sail - boat directions in relation to wind direction, i.e., close-hauled, beam reaching, broad reaching, and running.

Port - 1. - the left side of a boat when facing forward. 2. - a harbor. 3. - a window in a cabin on a boat.

Port tack - sailing on any point of sail with the main boom on the starboard side of the boat.

Prevailing wind - typical or consistent wind conditions.

Propane - a cooking fuel.

Propeller - a device, having a revolving hub with radiating blades, which is used for propulsion.

Puff - an increase in wind speed for a short duration.

Pulpit - a stainless steel guardrail at the bow and stern of some boats.

Pumpout station - location for legal emptying of holding tanks.

Pushpit - a stainless steel guardrail at the stern of some boats.

▶ Q (Quebec)

Q flag - solid yellow flag, designating request for pratique or clearance by officials.

Quadrant - connects rudder post to steering cables in wheel steering.

Quarter - the sides of the boat near the stern.

Quarter berth - a bunk located under the cockpit.

▶ R (Romeo)

Radar reflector - a metal object with lots of faces at sharp angles which can be spotted by other vessels' radar scopes.

Rake - the angle of the mast.

Range - the alignment of two objects that indicates the middle of a channel.

Raw-water - the fresh or salt water entering the boat.

Reach - one of several points of sail across the wind.

"Ready about" - the command given to the crew to prepare to tack.

"Ready to jibe" - the command given to the crew to prepare to jibe.

Reef - to reduce the size of a sail.

Reefing line - a line used to reduce sail by pulling the lower portion of the sail to the boom.

Reeve - to pass a line through a cringle or block.

Rhumb line - a straight course between two points.

Rig - 1. - the design of a boat's mast(s), standing rigging, and sail plan. 2. - to prepare a boat to go sailing.

Rigging - the wires and lines used to support and control sails.

Right-of-way - the right of the stand-on vessel to hold its course.

Roach - the sail area aft of a straight line running from the head to the clew of a sail.

Rode - line and chain attached from the boat to the anchor.

Roller furling - a mechanical system to roll up a headsail (jib) around the headstay.

Round up - when the boat turns, sometimes abruptly and with a great deal of heel, towards the wind.

Rudder - the underwater fin that is controlled by the wheel or tiller to deflect water and steer the boat.

Run - (point of sail) sailing with the wind coming behind the boat.

Running rigging - lines and hardware used to control the sails.

▶ S (Sierra)

Safety harness - strong webbing worn around the chest and attached to the boat to prevent someone from being separated from the boat.

Sail ties - pieces of line or webbing used to tie the mainsail to the boom when reefing or storing the sail.

Scope - the ratio of the amount of anchor rode deployed to the distance from the bow to the bottom.

Scull - to propel a boat by swinging the rudder back and forth like a fish tail.

Scupper - cockpit or deck drain.

Seabag - a soft fabric bag for carrying personal items.

Sea breeze - a wind that blows over the sea and onto the land.

Seacock - a valve which opens and closes a hole through the hull for salt water needed on board or discharge.

Secure - make safe or cleat.

Sécurite - an internationally recognized signal to warn others of a dangerous situation.

Set - 1. - the direction of a current. 2. - to trim the sails.

Shackle - a metal fitting at the end of a line used to attach the line to a sail or another fitting.

Shake out - to remove a reef and restore the full sail.

Sheave - the rotating wheel inside a block or fitting.

Sheet - the line which is used to control the sail by easing it out or trimming it in.

Shoal - shallow water that may be dangerous.

Shroud - standing rigging at the side of the mast.

S-Jibe - the controlled method of jibing with the mainsail crossing the boat under control and the boat's path makes an "S" shaped course.

Skeg - a vertical fin in front of the rudder.

Skipper - the person in charge of the boat.

Slab reefing (jiffy reefing) - lowering and tying off the lower portion of a sail in order to reduce sail area.

Slip - see **berth**.

Snub - to hold a line under tension by wrapping it on a winch or cleat.

Sole - the floor in a cockpit or cabin.

Solenoid switch - an electrical switch which shuts off the flow of propane.

Spar - a pole used to attach a sail on a boat, for example, the mast, the boom, a gaff.

Spinnaker - a large billowing headsail used when sailing downwind.

Splice - the joining of two lines together by interweaving their strands.

Spreader - a support strut extending athwartships from the mast used to support the mast and guide the shrouds from the top of the mast to the chainplates.

Spring line - a dockline running forward or aft from the boat to the dock to keep the boat from moving forward or aft.

Squall - a short intense storm with little warning.

Stanchions - stainless steel supports at the edge of the deck which hold the lifelines.

Standing rigging - the permanent rigging (usually wire) of a boat, including the forestay, backstay, and shrouds.

Stand-on vessel - the vessel or boat with the right-of-way.

Starboard - when looking from the stern toward the bow, the right side of the boat.

Starboard tack - sailing on any point of sail with the main boom on the port side of the boat.

Stay - a wire support for a mast, part of the standing rigging.

Staysail (STAY-sil) - on a cutter, a second small "inner jib," attached between the bow and the mast.

Steerageway - minimum amount of speed needed to control direction of vessel.

Stem - the forward tip of the bow.

Step - the area in which the base of the mast fits.

Stern - the aft part of the boat.

Stuffing box (packing gland) - the opening in the hull where the propeller shaft exits.

Sump - a cavity or tank in the bilge to collect water.

▶ T (Tango)

Tack - 1. - a course on which the wind comes over one side of the boat, i.e., port tack, starboard tack. 2. - to change direction by turning the bow through the wind. 3. - the lower forward corner of a sail.

Tackle - a sequence of blocks and line that provides a mechanical advantage.

Tail - to hold and pull a line from behind a winch.

Telltales - pieces of yarn or sailcloth material attached to sails which indicate when the sail is properly trimmed.

Tether - length of line connecting safety harness to padeye or jackline.

Throttle - a device for controlling the engine's revolutions per minute (RPM).

Tide - the rise and fall of water level due to the gravitational pull of the sun and moon.

Toe rail - a short aluminum or wooden rail around the outer edges of the deck.

Toppinglift - a line used to hold the boom up when the mainsail is lowered or stowed.

Topsides - the sides of the boat between the waterline and the deck.

Transom - the vertical surface of the stern.

Traveler - a track or bridle that controls sideways (athwartships) movement of the mainsail.

Trim - 1. - to pull in on a sheet. 2. - how a sail is set relative to the wind.

True wind - the actual speed and direction of the wind when standing still.

Tune - to adjust a boat's standing rigging.

Turnbuckle - a mechanical fitting attached to the lower ends of stays used to adjust the standing rigging.

▶ U (Uniform)

Underway - to be moving under sail or engine.

Upwind - toward the direction of the wind.

USCG - abbreviation for United States Coast Guard.

▶ V (Victor)

Vang - see **boom vang**.

Vee-berth - a bunk in the bow of the boat that narrows as it goes forward.

Veer - a clockwise change of wind direction.

Vessel - any sailboat, powerboat or ship.

VHF- abbreviation for Very High Frequency, a two-way radio commonly used for boating.

▶ W (Whiskey)

Wake - waves caused by a boat moving through the water.

Warping - to move a vessel by hauling on a line made fast to a dock, piling, anchor, pier or other stationary object.

Waterline - the horizontal line on the hull of a boat where the water surface should be.

Weather helm - the boat's tendency to head up toward the wind, which occurs when a sailboat is overpowered or the sail trim is out of balance (jib trim too loose and/or mainsail trim too tight).

Weather side - see **windward side**.

Whip - to bind together the strands at the end of a line.

Whisker pole - a pole, temporarily mounted between the mast and the clew of a jib, used to hold the jib out and keep it full when sailing downwind.

White caps - waves with foam tops.

Winch - a drum with a handle offering mechanical advantage used to trim sheets or raise sails.

Windage - the amount of surface area, including sails, rigging and hull, that's presented to the wind.

Windward - toward the wind.

Windward side - the side of a boat or a sail closest to the wind.

Wing-and-wing - sailing downwind with the jib set on the opposite side of the mainsail.

Working sails - the mainsail and standard jib.

Working sheet - the leeward jib sheet that is tensioned by the wind on the sail.

▶ X (X-Ray)

▶ Y (Yankee)

Y-valve - a double valve used to redirect water flow.

▶ Z (Zulu)

Information and Regulatory Markers
(Gold)

Chart Symbols

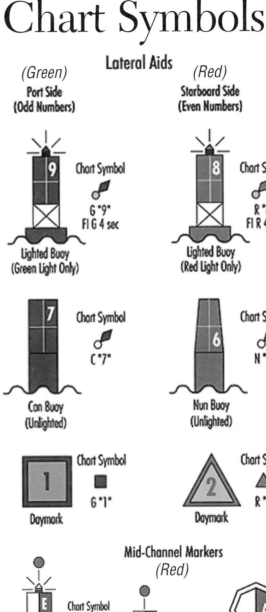

Lateral Aids

(Green)
Port Side
(Odd Numbers)

(Red)
Starboard Side
(Even Numbers)

Chart Symbol
G "9"
Fl G 4 sec

Chart Symbol
R "8"
Fl R 4 sec

Lighted Buoy
(Green Light Only)

Lighted Buoy
(Red Light Only)

Chart Symbol
C "7"

Chart Symbol
N "6"

Can Buoy
(Unlighted)

Nun Buoy
(Unlighted)

Chart Symbol
G "1"

Chart Symbol
R "2"

Daymark

Daymark

Mid-Channel Markers
(Red)

Chart Symbol
RW "E"
Mo (A)

Chart Symbol
RW
C "E"

MR
Chart Symbol

RW
"A"

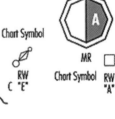
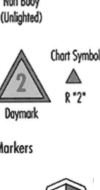

ROCK

Diamond Shape
warns of danger

5
MPH

Circle marks
area controlled
"as indicated"

MULLET LAKE
BLACK RIVER

For displaying information
such as directions,
distances, locations, etc.

Diamond Shape
with cross means
boats keep out

US SAILING Bareboat Cruising Certification

The Bareboat Cruising graduate will have successfully demonstrated the ability to skipper and crew an inboard auxiliary powered cruising sailboat within sight of land and bring it safely to anchor during daylight hours.

Recommended Equipment: It is recommended that Bareboat Cruising courses and examinations be conducted on 30' to 45' sloop-rigged cruising keelboats with wheel steering and auxiliary diesel power, and with adequate equipment inventory to complete all required certification outcomes.

Prerequisite: The prerequisite for Bareboat Cruising Certification is Basic Cruising Certification.

Certification Requirements: Bareboat Cruising Certification requires the successful completion of the following knowledge and skill requirements. These requirements are expected to be able to be performed safely with confident command of the boat with a wind of at least 15 knots.

Practical Skills

Preparation to Sail:
1. Obtain an appropriate weather forecast for your cruise and plan accordingly.
2. Check the sail inventory and select the appropriate sails for the conditions.
3. Check the location and condition or operation of all safety equipment.
4. Describe the need for and perform the daily checks of the engine fluids and mechanical parts, manual and electric bilge pumps, and the electrical, mechanical, fresh water, marine head and holding tank systems.
5. Perform a complete check and demonstrate safe use of the galley stove and stove fuel system.
6. Ensure that all necessary provisions, cooking and eating utensils are aboard and properly stowed.
7. Check the security and operation of all hatches, ports and companionways.
8. Inventory and check the condition of all bimini tops, cockpit awnings and dodgers where applicable.
9. Inventory and check the condition of all tools and spare parts.
10. Check the condition of dinghy and oars (and outboard, if applicable).
11. Inventory and check the condition of all required charts, tide tables, cruising guides and navigation tools.
12. Perform a complete inspection of all deck gear: standing and running rigging, lifelines, stanchions and pulpits.
13. Understand your responsibilities and liabilities as a bareboat charter customer according to your contract with your charter company.

Crew Operations and Skills:
14. Demonstrate a comprehensive crew briefing and plan of responsibilities.
15. Demonstrate the operation of the emergency steering equipment.

Leaving the Dock or Mooring:
16. Demonstrate the proper lashing of a dinghy on deck or securing it for towing.
17. Demonstrate appropriate helmsman and crew coordination and the skills necessary for leaving under power in any wind condition.

Navigation (Piloting):
18. Demonstrate your ability to: correctly use a handbearing compass and a ship's compass; maintain a proper DR plot with time/speed/distance calculations; work up an estimated position; plot a fix using lines of position and/or ranges; use depth soundings; use accepted plotting and labeling techniques; understand buoyage systems and aids to navigation;identify and correlate visual observations and landmarks with chart symbols.
19. Understand the fundamental operation of a Loran or GPS to locate a position of latitude and longitude.
Heavy Weather Sailing:
20. Demonstrate shortening sail to depower, and explain effects on balancing the boat.
21. Demonstrate heaving-to.

Overboard Recovery Methods:
22. Properly demonstrate one of the overboard recovery methods under sail, which is most appropriate for: your sailing ability, boat type, crew experience, wind and sea conditions, and maintaining constant visual contact with the victim.
23. Demonstrate an overboard recovery method under power which allows you to maintain visual contact with the victim.

Anchoring Techniques
24. Select an anchorage and demonstrate appropriate helmsman and crew coordination and the skills necessary to anchor with two anchors under power using one of the following methods: bow and stern, two anchors off the bow at 60∞, or two anchors off the bow at 180∞ (Bahamian Moor).
25. Pick up a mooring.
26. Demonstrate appropriate helmsman and crew coordination and the skills necessary to recover your anchor under power.

Returning to the Dock or Mooring:

27. Demonstrate appropriate helmsman and crew coordination and the skills necessary for returning to the dock under power in any wind direction.

Securing the Boat Properly:

28. Demonstrate the correct procedure for returning the charter boat in the same condition that it was chartered, and complete a charter check-in report on the condition of the boat.

Knowledge

Preparation to Sail:

1. Understand bareboat charter procedures and responsibilities for both the charter company and the charter client.
2. Determine the vessel's fuel capacity, fuel consumption, and cruising range under power.
3. Be familiar with the documentation required for the vessel and crew both nationally and internationally.
4. Be familiar with the legal responsibilities of a skipper and the courtesies to be observed when entering a foreign port.
5. Understand the legal responsibilities of the overboard discharge of pollutants.
6. Understand all federal, state and local regulations as they pertain to your boat.
7. Be familiar with all required documentation for crew and vessel nationally and internationally.

Crew Operations and Skills:

8. Understand how to safely go aloft and explain the reasons for doing so.
9. Describe commonly observed nautical etiquette when cruising in foreign waters.
10. Be familiar with proper rafting techniques at docks and at anchor.

Navigation (Piloting):

11. Understand how to: use tide and tidal current tables including secondary station predictions; use the rule of twelfths; and apply set and drift and anticipated leeway when determining a course to steer.
12. Understand the correct use of a ship's log.
13. Be familiar with the considerations, responsibilities and special techniques required for navigation in restricted visibility.
14. Understand the meaning of the visual observations of water color.
15. Be familiar with the use of such navigation publications as charts, cruising guides, Coast Pilots and Light Lists.

Heavy Weather Sailing:

16. Describe the signs of an approaching squall and the actions to be taken.
17. Describe the safety issues involved with heaving to.

Overboard Recovery Methods;

18. Be familiar with the equipment provided for overboard recovery.
19. Understand procedures for overboard recovery in a larger cruising boat in unfamiliar waters and with a crew that you might not sail with regularly. Understand the Quick-Stop, Lifesling-type and Quick-Turn overboard recovery methods under sail to include: constant visual contact with the victim, communications, recovery plan, sequence of maneuvers, boathandling, course sailed, pickup approach, and coming alongside the victim (or simulated object).
20. Describe methods of getting an overboard recovery victim back on deck after the vessel is stopped alongside.
21. Explain when overboard recovery should be done under power and the inherent dangers.

Safety and Emergency Procedures:

22. Giving due consideration to the state of the tide, describe a plan of action if you run aground in moderate conditions.
23. Describe a plan of action if your vessel has: a broken thru-hull; been holed; an engine failure; a steering failure.

Anchoring Techniques:

24. Describe the procedures for anchoring with two anchors.
25. Describe the use of a tripline/anchor buoy.
26. Describe the procedures for clearing fouled anchor rodes, and for recovering an anchor from under another boat.
27. Describe the procedures for dealing with a dragged anchor.
28. Describe the advantages and disadvantages of the following anchoring methods: bow and stern, two anchors off the bow at 60°, two anchors off the bow at 180° (Bahamian Moor), and Mediterranean moor.

Returning to the Dock or Mooring:

29. Describe the precautions when docking under sail.

Securing the Boat Properly:

30. Describe the responsibilities of the charter client and the charter company when returning the boat.

An introduction to US SAILING.

Since 1897 the United States Sailing Association (US SAILING) has provided support for American sailors at all levels of sailing — in all kinds of sailboats. The primary objective of its Training Program is to provide a national standard of quality instruction for all people learning to sail. The US SAILING Keelboat Certification System includes a series of books such as *Bareboat Cruising*, a program of student certifications and an extensive educational and training program for instructors. It is one of the most highly developed and effective national training systems for students and sailing instructors and is recognized nationally and internationally.

US SAILING is a non-profit organization and the official National Governing Body of Sailing as designated by the U. S. Congress in the Amateur Sports Act. It has a national Training Program for sailors in dinghies, windsurfers, multihulls and keelboats. It is also the official representative to the International Sailing Federation (ISAF).

The US SAILING Keelboat Certification System is designed to develop safe, responsible and confident sailors who meet specific performance and knowledge standards. (See US SAILING BAREBOAT CRUISING Certification on page 108 for the BAREBOAT CRUISING standards.) There are other benefits for you as well. You can start at the BASIC KEELBOAT certification level and progress through BASIC CRUISING, BAREBOAT CRUISING, COASTAL NAVIGATION, and even go on to COASTAL PASSAGE MAKING, CELESTIAL NAVIGATION and OFFSHORE PASSAGE MAKING. With your US SAILING certifications and experience documented in the *Official Logbook of Sailing*, you will have a passport to cruising and chartering boats locally or worldwide.

Bareboat Cruising is intended as a supplement to your sailing lessons, rather than as a substitute for them. It was created to help you accelerate your learning curve and clarify your understanding of the concepts and techniques of sailing and cruising.

What Makes Sailing Special?
The sport of sailing is open to people of all ages, incomes and abilities. Sailing offers virtually limitless choices of boats, each with its own unique characteristics, and the opportunity to explore an adjacent cove or an exotic tropical location.

Most sailors will acquire entry-level skills quite rapidly. Mastering those skills is an experience that will be rewarding, exciting and pleasurable for a lifetime.

As you continue to sail, you will find that sailing is more than simply being pushed and pulled by the wind. For most people, sailing is meeting new friends, enjoying nature's beauty and challenge, and sharing a unique fellowship with all boaters. A tremendous camaraderie exists among sailors, particularly on the water, which makes sailing — and the people who do it — very special.

What can US SAILING do for you?

US SAILING is committed to helping you discover and enjoy the beauty, relaxation, challenge and friendships of sailing. As part of this commitment we offer:

THE KEELBOAT CERTIFICATION SYSTEM with its various levels of training and certification:

■ **Basic Keelboat.** To responsibly skipper and crew a simple daysailing keelboat in familiar waters in light to moderate wind and sea conditions.

■ **Basic Cruising.** To responsibly skipper and crew an auxiliary powered cruising sailboat during daylight hours within sight of land in moderate wind and sea conditions.

■ **Bareboat Cruising**. To responsibly skipper, crew or bareboat charter an inboard auxiliary powered cruising sailboat within sight of land to a port or an anchorage during daylight hours in moderate to strong wind and sea conditions.

■ **Coastal Navigation.** To properly use traditional navigation techniques and electronic navigation for near coastal passage making.

■ **Coastal Passage Making.** To responsibly skipper and crew an inboard auxiliary powered cruising sailboat for coastal or offshore passages in strong to heavy conditions, including zero visibility and nighttime, in unfamiliar waters out of sight of land.

■ **Celestial Navigation.** To navigate using celestial techniques and integrating celestial with traditional navigation techniques.

■ **Offshore Passage Making.** To responsibly skipper and crew an inboard auxiliary powered cruising sailboat to any destination worldwide.

THE BASIC WINDSURFING CERTIFICATION which is available for entry level sailors.

THE SMALL BOAT CERTIFICATION SYSTEM which is available for dinghy, daysailer and multihull sailors in two wind speed ranges: light and heavy air.

Plus many other useful services:

US SAILING certified instructors help you achieve new skills and knowledge using up to date and safe methods.

Course materials, including this book, presented in a highly visual format to help you gain competency and confidence in your sailing skills and knowledge.

The Official Logbook of Sailing, recognized nationally and internationally, to document your US SAILING certifications and experience and use as a passport to chartering boats locally and worldwide.

A national database so charter companies can confirm your sailing credentials.

A list of sailing schools that use US SAILING certified instructors and US SAILING course materials.

US SAILING Safety-at-Sea seminars.

U.S. Coast Guard recognition of the completion of a safe boating course, often one of the requirements for licensing.

Racing Rules and handicap rating systems.

US SAILING membership makes you a part of the National Governing Body for the Sport of Sailing and the recipient of a free one-year subscription to a major sailing magazine as well as discounts on products and services.

www.ussailing.org

A Special
Acknowledgement to
Sail America

US SAILING would like to thank Sail America for their continuing support of quality sailing instruction and the grant they provided to help publish this book. Sail America was founded in 1990 to represent all segments of the sailing industry — from boat builders to sailing schools — with the mission of increasing public interest in sailing and expanding the sailing market. Sail America's mission: "Promoting the Growth of the Sailing Industry."

Today Sail America, in affiliation with the NMMA, produces 5 of the country's top ALL-SAIL boatshows including:

SAIL EXPO — November, St. Petersburg, FL

Atlantic SAIL EXPO — January, Atlantic City, NJ

Strictly Sail — late January / early February, Chicago, IL

Strictly Sail — February, Miami, FL

Pacific SAIL EXPO — April, Oakland, CA

SAIL AMERICA reinvests the proceeds from these shows into several important programs to help stimulate interest in sailing. These programs include:

Discover Sailing, a marketing outreach program designed to encourage new comers to try sailing as well as making it easier for them to get involved. This program includes free introductory sails at various events, a comprehensive sailing introduction video and *discoversailing.com*.

Public relations featuring the *John Southam Award*. This annual award encourages journalists to help promote the sailing lifestyle and each recognizes those who do the best job of doing so.

Government relations, through a contribution to the NMMA, the industry associations work together to influence policy to make boating safer, easier and more fun for the boating public.

For information about Sail America and access to their membership database comprised of the 650 leading sailing industry businesses that seek to make sailing the most enjoyable activity possible, please visit HYPERLINK "http://www.sailamerica.com" www.sailamerica.com.